Kathy Run

Growing Up Under the Big Sky

KATHY RICE

Inks and Bindings
888-290-5218
www.inksandbindings.com
orders@inksandbindings.com

Contents

Foreword

By Carolyn Hink, Sister to author, Kathy Rice

Once upon a time (that's how Mom would always begin our bedtime stories) Mom and Dad sat at the dinner table in their tiny 3 room home on the windswept prairie with their four young children. The oldest, the only girl (me, Carolyn Hink), had just been moved into her own room., the old pantry just off the kitchen, while the youngest of the three boys, Johnny, had just been moved out of the living room where Mom and Dad slept on a pull-out sofa, and into the little bedroom with his brothers. Mom and Dad had an important question to ask: "What would you say to us having another baby?" The four of us looked at one another and in total agreement exclaimed in all seriousness, "There isn't room for another baby!"

The subject was dropped until another day. The next time we weren't asked, but were told that we would be getting a new baby! And because we weren't asked, we were overjoyed! Another baby! Right away I put my order in for a little sister! I absolutely HAD to be a girl! Three little brothers were plenty for me!

Time passed, and one January evening it was determined that it was time. Dad put all of us kids in the back seat of the old Chevy station wagon and helped Mom into the front seat. This was in the days before fathers were allowed in the delivery room, and children under the age of 12 were not allowed inside the hospital at all except as a patient. That meant that we had to remain in the dark in the car parked in front of the Daniels Memorial Hospital and wait while Dad helped Mom get settled.

How I wanted to be in there with her! I wanted to be the first to see my new baby sister! (Of course, that was also back in the dark ages before ultrasound technology so we had no way of knowing for sure she was a girl…)

Dad finally came back to the car, drove us back home to the farm and put us to bed. This was only a few months after our house received telephone service, so Dad eagerly waited all night long for the phone to ring because he had made the doctor promise to call as soon as the baby was born. Kathryn Lynn Rustebakke made her way into the world in the middle of the night, but the phone remained silent. Just before sending us off to school the next morning, Dad learned that he had a new baby daughter – the doctor had somehow decided that Dad had gone to bed and shouldn't have his sleep disturbed with the news! Dad was not happy about that, but delighted to have another beautiful child.

Because of the rule about children not being allowed to visit the hospital if under the age of 12, I had to wait almost an entire week before getting to see this precious new sister, but one day when I came home from school, there she was! That picture is permanently etched in my mind; she was in the old blue buggy Mom used as a bassinet, near the oil stove in the living room, all bundled up and fast asleep and cute as a baby can be. Kathy Run was now part of our family.

By Carolyn Hink

Chapter 1
Harvest Time

The warm summer days were almost over. Eight-year-old Johnny and I knelt in our favorite spot, the "hole." It was a former well near our house filled in with soil and kept clear of the weeds and brown dry grass that blanketed the rest of the never-ending prairie. It was filled with the same sandy soil that my father depended on to grow the hard red spring wheat on our northeastern Montana farm. The soil made a good sand box where my brother and I spent hours creating cities and long rural roads.

As I pushed and scooped the dirt here and there with my little hands, Johnny meticulously graded and formed his highways with the Tonka® road graders, steam shovels, and tractors he carefully protected from his little sister's careless hands. Johnny was my hero. He was three years older than me, and everything he said was so.

"School starts next week," he stated. He didn't sound thrilled, but I was bursting with anticipation. I was five-and-a-half, and my parents had obtained special permission for me to start first grade this year in the little one room school house at Four Buttes. I could hardly wait! Carolyn and David, my older sister and brother, were already in high school. Paul, my middle brother, was in seventh grade. They were all a year ahead of the other pupils in their classes. David and Carolyn had each skipped a grade.

The little library nook in the one-room country school held text books as well as the regular library books. During reading time, when the teacher was working with other grades, my brother and sister had gone to the library and read the text books. When the teacher couldn't find any text books for their grades that they hadn't already completed, she had no choice except to put them a grade ahead.

Now I came along, entering a year early, not because of my superior intelligence or abilities, but simply because five other students were starting this year, and none next year. My parents were concerned that I would have no peers to share my school experience with, so they got permission to let me start four months before my sixth birthday.

I watched Johnny bank the road so the imaginary driver could take the corner faster, just like on the race tracks and on the gravel road beyond our lane. This road led to Shipstead's farm house. Young drivers boasted they could take that corner at 50 miles an hour, and we figured that was good engineering on the part of the road construction crew.

"Kathy and Johnny! Let's take dinner out to the field," my mother called.

Aunt Selma, Grandpa's sister, was visiting from Thief River Falls, Minnesota, and out-of-town guests always made any day seem like a holiday.

The wheat stood tall and golden, and the huge combine sliced through it as it circled the field. The combine threshers shook the incoming stalks of wheat, separating the grain from the straw. The kernels then fell into the auger that carried them up to the hopper, where they remained until they could be emptied into the back of Daddy's truck.

Wheat Harvest

"Pure gold." That's what my dad called the grain. Half our year's income was falling, jumping, sifting, and bouncing its way through that noisy, wonderful giant of a machine we called a combine. It was exciting to go to the field at harvest time. My father and grandfather were in high spirits while harvesting their crop, but they worked long hours to take advantage of good weather. A sudden hail storm could destroy the unharvested crop, and rainy weather could cause long delays and lower the quality of the wheat. Sometimes, when the wheat was late in ripening or when wet weather caused long delays, they had to work all night to get the grain harvested before snow covered the ground. Morning dew often caused delays because wheat has to be dry to be combined. We all did what we could to help.

Mom wrote for the weekly newspaper in town, but during harvest she put her newspaper writing on hold. She made dinners at noon and lunches at four o'clock. The men came in for supper around ten at night. There was no time to write articles for the paper because she was needed to bake breads and pies and be home just to be available as an extra driver to move equipment from one field to the next. She was willing to drop everything to make a quick run to town for machinery repairs if needed.

Grandpa handled the auger that lifted the newly-harvested grain from the truck into the steel bin or the old wooden granaries over at Grandpa's old place. They stored the grain there until grain prices were up and he could sell it.

Eleven-year-old Paul and thirteen-year-old David took turns driving the truck. Carolyn, who was fourteen, preferred to enjoy the harvest scene from the back of her horse whenever possible.

Johnny and I jumped in the back seat of the 1953 Chevy station wagon, disregarding the fact that we were covered with dirt and sand. Aunt Selma slipped into the front seat as Mom and Carolyn put the boxes filled with dinner in the back and closed the tailgate. We sat in the back seat with Carolyn as Mom drove down the trail to the field. Most of daddy's fields were close to home, but today he was in a field three miles away. We told Aunt Selma our favorite jokes.

"Wanna hear a dirty joke?" We giggled. "Pig fell in a mud puddle."

Aunt Selma laughed a hearty laugh, and returned, "Knock-knock."

"Who's there?"

"The little old lady."

"The little old lady who?"

"Well, I didn't know you could yodel!" she exclaimed.

We drove over some slight hills and squealed as our "bellies did flips." We were convinced that this was the next best thing to the carnival that had been in town a couple weeks earlier.

The late summer prairie was fragrant with wild flowers and freshly harvested fields. Bluebells and buttercups dotted the hills, sage brush filled in the coulees, and deep yellow sunflowers lined the dusty trail. We watched out the side windows to see if we could catch sight of a gopher or badger. The land wasn't populated like it was in the "olden days," with buffalo and elk, but there were plenty of deer, ground squirrels, skunks, and porcupines.

Grandpa and Paul waited in the truck at the end of the field. They were happy to see us. Any break from the heat, mosquitoes, dust, and boredom was welcomed, especially if it included Mom's good home cooked meal.

My father wasn't one to enjoy picnics. Mom said his time in the army was like a four-year picnic, and he avoided any reminder of the war. Now he preferred eating at the kitchen table with chairs, a strong electric fan and no bugs.

I climbed into the cab of the truck where my brother Paul was reading a stack of comic books.

"Will you show me how to shift gears?" I asked.

He finished the last page of his Archie comic book and set it on the dash.

"Okay," he began patiently, "this is neutral. When the truck is in neutral, it doesn't go anywhere."

I wiggled the loose gear shift and asked, "What good is neutral then?"

"Well, you need neutral so you can shift from one gear to the next," he explained. "And if you're waiting for Dad to empty the truck, you can sit with the truck idling. The truck doesn't run off when it's in neutral, but you hafta use the emergency brake so it doesn't roll."

I practiced moving the gear shift to second, third, fourth gear and back through each gear to first. Paul coached me through the paces. Once I learned to shift, Daddy might let me drive for harvest, I reasoned. Daddy already let me sit on his lap and steer when he drove on the back lane.

Aunt Selma helped Mom set up the double-sized metal table and cover it with a red and white checkered oil cloth. Carolyn and Grandpa helped Mom set out the potatoes, gravy, tender roast beef, hot fresh corn on the cob, tubs of home-churned butter, homemade pies, and a couple half-gallon canning jars with icy grape Kool-Aid. The noon meal was always the biggest, even when it had to be transported out to the field.

Harvest Dinner

The farmers practiced strip farming on these windblown dry plains. In the distance the entire countryside looked like sleeping tigers, with the strips of golden wheat alternating with strips of dark brown soil.

The roar of the combine and the rhythm of the interactive moving parts brought my attention to the field. I watched as the combine climbed the last hill. First the tall auger appeared, dumping the wheat into the hopper. Then I could see Daddy and my oldest brother David. David drove while Daddy flattened the wheat in the hopper with a stick, much like Mom did with a table knife when she leveled flour as she measured it while making bread.

Daddy kept careful records of the crop yield from field to field and year to year, and he was measuring the bushels he got on this round. We had had plenty of rain this year, and the crop yield was good.

Paul started the truck and I put it into first gear. He pulled up close to the combine, under the auger spout.

David jumped off the massive machine, and quickly grabbed a plate of food as the wheat poured into the box of the truck. It wasn't often Daddy let him take the combine on a solo run, but the combine had to keep going, and with Aunt Selma here, Daddy decided David could make one round alone.

When the hopper was empty Daddy and Grandpa sat in the shade of the truck and enjoyed the fine meal with Aunt Selma and Mom while David took the combine around the field alone. Johnny, Paul, and I ate quickly, and as the adults visited, we chased grasshoppers and played tag.

By the time the grownups finished their pie and whipped cream David was back from making the round. Daddy excused himself so he could measure the wheat from this round. As the hopper emptied into the back of the truck, Johnny and I helped Mom gather up the empty dishes and load the station wagon. When we reached home, Johnny and I helped Mom and Aunt Selma carry the boxes of empty dishes to the house. They cleaned the kitchen and washed the dishes.

Johnny and I followed Carolyn to the barnyard. She held a carrot in the palm of her hand, trying to lure her pinto pony within her grasp. She finally cornered Patch and slipped the reins around his neck and tried to get the bit past his clenched teeth. Patch foolishly decided to risk it all for the carrot that she held in her hand with the bit. She slipped the bit into his mouth and fastened the bridle as he munched noisily on his carrot. Carolyn jumped on his bare back with no saddle for her afternoon ride.

During the long days of seeding and harvest Mom always prepared afternoon lunches for the men. Today she made my favorite, liverwurst sandwiches with soft, white, homemade bread. Aunt Selma wrapped them in waxed paper. At four o'clock we were off to the field again with the sandwiches, chilled watermelon, and ice-cold pop, so cold ice crystals had formed in the necks of the bottles. This satisfied the appetites of the hungry working men until they quit working late at night.

Around ten p.m., tired, dirty, and hungry, the men washed in the basin in the entry and sat down to a macaroni casserole, vegetables, and assorted leftovers. Aunt Selma and Grandpa reminisced with Daddy about harvest time when Daddy was a little boy. In those days they used a horse-drawn binder that wrapped the wheat in bundles. Later, the steam-powered threshing machine would separate the straw and chaff from the kernels. We still used the old binder for harvesting oats, but Daddy used his Minneapolis-Moline tractor instead of horses to pull it, and the combine replaced the cumbersome threshing machine.

Chapter 2
School Days

Mom knew how to take advantage of the "Back-to-School" sales. Selections were limited in our hometown, Scobey, so we also made expeditions to two neighboring towns. Plentywood had two full blocks of dress shops, shoe stores, variety stores, and other shops. Wolf Point had even more. We made a trip to Plentywood one week, and the next week we drove to Wolf Point. Both "cities" were about fifty miles away, and we planned on a full day of shopping at each town. Since these towns were so big, we found everything we needed, and if we didn't find it, Daddy said we didn't need it.

When we returned home, I placed my new clothes in a dresser drawer or hung them in the closet, where they remained untouched until the first day of school.

When the first day of school finally came, harvest was almost over and the visitors we had enjoyed throughout the summer had all gone home. I had to decide which new dress I would wear. I wanted to wear all of them. Finally, I decided on my new rust colored plaid jumper with a white blouse.

The older children could buy hot lunches at the big school in Scobey, but we younger ones had to carry our own lunches to the Four Buttes School. Mom packed Johnny and my lunch buckets with my favorite tuna fish sandwiches, a thermos of Campbell's bean soup, a banana and two homemade sugar cookies for each of us.

We sat down to a breakfast of French toast, sausage, and orange juice. As soon as we finished, we scrambled outside for pictures. I stood next to Johnny with my new treasure chest lunch box as Mom snapped a photo of our stair-step family. We stood, oldest to youngest, shortest to tallest, me, Johnny, Paul, David and last of all, Carolyn. How I wanted a baby sister or brother! Nevertheless, Mom said she had just the family she always wanted, so I should have my own babies some day when I grow up.

1st Day of School

The days were becoming cooler and the fields had turned golden brown. The tree leaves were beginning to turn color. I was happy to finally say goodbye to summer.

The school bus drove up the lane and we waved goodbye to Mom and greeted the bus driver and our friends.

As the little bus pulled up to the Four Buttes Mercantile, the general store close to the one-room school, we saw the "big bus" waiting to take the older children to the big school in Scobey. David and Paul ran into the store to purchase nickel candy bars and a couple pencils before getting on the big bus. I waved as they found their seats and the bus pulled away from the sidewalk and crossed the train tracks on the way to the highway.

Johnny and I walked with the rest of the children beyond the store and past Mr. Johnson's garden and garage to the one-room school.

The teacher had already raised the flag on the tall flagpole by the schoolhouse. The flag chain gently slapped against the pole as the flag waved high above our heads in the gentle breeze. A white picket fence graced the front of the school yard, and a row of swings, teeters and a high slide stood in the playground at the side.

As I entered the little white building, I felt big. I was a first grader, and my best friend, Kristi, was there, too. Her birthday was the beginning of September, so she would soon be six. I was the only five-year-old in school.

The girls' restroom was on the right and the boys' restroom was on the left as we entered the front door.

Straight ahead was the entry, the room we called the hall. Two walls were lined with enough lockers so we could each have our own. Hanging in the middle of the hall was a thick hemp rope that, when pulled, rang the heavy bell in the bell tower on top of the school. It rang five times a day, calling us to school in the morning, back after lunch, morning and afternoon recesses, and one last time when school was over for the day. I figured the last bell was to warn the whole village that we were coming.

The old wooden desks in the classroom were lined according to grade levels. The little desks for the first graders were on the left, next to the windows. There were no second graders this year, so the third graders were next to us. The larger desks where the older children sat were on the other side of the room near the chalkboard. The green chalkboard stretched across the entire front of the classroom and most of the side wall opposite the windows. At the end of the chalkboard on the side wall was a bulletin board decorated beautifully with back-to-school decorations. Above that was a large clock. In the back corner was the library nook, a room like an open closet with shelves lining the three walls from the floor almost to the ceiling.

The teacher's desk was in front of the room, facing the students' desks. On top sat five shiny red apples presented by hopeful teacher's pets. To the right of the teacher's desk was a door leading into the tiny teacherage, where occasionally a teacher would choose to stay during a school year. It contained a tiny sink-refrigerator-range combination, a twin-sized bed, and a small table with two chairs. A first aid kit and a black dial telephone hung on the wall. A door led to the back entry where the basement stairs were located.

After the teacher, Mrs. Trang, showed us where we were to sit, we waited quietly to hear the rules. All the first graders' moms came in to make sure we were all right. The teacher addressed all of us, and when she finished, we each kissed our mother goodbye. Then the four first grade girls went to the bathroom.

"I think she's nice," Kristi said, discretely fanning her dress over her legs as she sat on the commode.

Acrobatic Elinor hung upside down by her knees on the divider between the toilet and the sink. Ellen and I splashed in the sink, and we all agreed that we were going to like first grade.

Suddenly the lavatory door flung open and an angry Mrs. Trang yelled, "What do you think you're doing? It's time for school! You can't just leave the room when you feel like it! You must raise your hand and ask permission! This is first grade! One more stunt like that, and there will be no recess for you!"

Well, so much for our first impression of our teacher! She was mean! I was devastated! Nobody told us first grade was going to be so hard! We filed into the classroom as our big brothers and sisters looked on us with protective pity.

We first graders had three things in common. Most of us came from fairly large families, we each had a big brother or sister in third grade, and we were each the youngest in our families, except for the Dahl sisters, who had a baby brother. Kristi, like me, was the youngest of five children. Steve, her oldest brother, went to the big school with my big brothers and sister, but the rest of her family still attended the little one room school. Her sister Penny was in Johnny's grade. Her brother Jimmy was in fourth grade, and her sister, Onalee, was a sixth grader.

Ellen and Elinor, with auburn hair, were sisters who looked like twins. There were six children in their family and Monte, their older brother, was in the same grade as Johnny. Elinor had missed so much school because of illness the previous year that she had to start first grade over. Mike was the youngest of three children, and his big sister, Candy, was Johnny's classmate, too. Ray was in my class for our first-grade year, but he and his brother, Alan, who was in Johnny's class moved away by the next year. There were two or three sixth graders and a couple fourth and fifth graders this year, but we were the little kids. We all looked up to them.

We all breathed a sigh of relief when morning recess finally arrived. Nobody had gotten into any more trouble. Mrs. Trang sat at her desk as we filed out of the building. The children split up into their various circles of friends.

Kristi talked the three girls in first grade into playing "horse" with her. We played around an old granary just beyond the far end of the schoolyard. Kristi was "Fury," her favorite horse on television. My family didn't have a television set, so I didn't know who I should be

"What sex do you want to be?" Kristi inquired.

"What do you mean?" I asked.

"You know, male or female?"

"Huh?" I queried, confused by her unfamiliar words.

"Do you want to be a stallion or a mare?"

Still no understanding.

"A stud or a brood?"

I didn't want to look stupid, but I had no idea what she was talking about!

"All right," she conceded, "Do you want to be a boy horse or a girl horse?"

By the time I decided to be a girl horse the heavy bell clanged and we ran to drink from the water fountain and find our seats before Mrs. Trang began our next lesson. Fury would have to wait until lunch.

Lunch time finally came. We had to wash our hands before we ate, so the girls filed into the girls' lavatory, and the boys into theirs. The older girls washed their hands and returned to their desks, as did the boys. The third-grade girls, Candy and Penny, were soaping up their hands, and invited us to join them. Six little girls slipped the soap around until we formed softly whipped dollops of suds. Over and over, we folded, stroked, and rubbed our hands so they became soft and shriveled, and very, very clean.

We were free to talk and laugh, even to trade parts of our lunches. I liked my own lunch, so although my school mates offered raisins, store-bought cookies, and peanut butter sandwiches, I declined politely and ate the feast my mother had prepared for me.

After we returned our lunch pails to our lockers, we went outside for the remainder of the hour. The other girls decided to play tag with the bigger kids, so Kristi and I joined the fun. We ran and laughed until the heavy bell tolled again, calling us to line up for drinks at the water fountain and go back to our seats.

Teacher gave us our "Pasting Pages" book. This book had pages of pictures we were to cut out and paste in the appropriate spots. At the beginning of the book, we simply matched shapes. But later there were letters to match with letters, pictures to match with letters, and finally words to match with pictures. This became our most dreaded workbook. It was the one book the teacher could bring out to discipline us when we were naughty. She knew how much we disliked it.

After we finished our Pasting Pages, Mrs. Trang told us the library rules. Only when we finished our work, when she was with another class, could we go to the three-sided nook and choose a book. We weren't to touch the construction paper that she stored on the bottom shelf.

The first-grade books were on the second shelf, and the other books were arranged so that the chapter books for the sixth graders were on the top shelf. Only two children could go to the library at a time, and there was to be no talking.

When we came in from the final recess it was time for our school meeting. Onalee, Kristi's oldest sister who was in sixth grade, had been school president last year. She called the meeting to order, and we proceeded to nominate and elect school officials. Cleaning the school was up to all of us, so in addition to voting on president, vice-president, secretary and treasurer, we voted for the librarian who would keep the books in order, a girls' restroom janitor, boys' restroom janitor, chalkboard janitor, trash burner and hall janitor. There were enough positions so that everyone got nominated and elected for some position, and enough positions to keep our school nice and tidy. Jimmy, Kristi's fourth grade brother, was to burn the trash. Johnny and Alan were elected to care for the flag.

It was time to go home, so Johnny and Alan went out to get the flag. Monte went into the hall and rode the rope up and down as he pulled and pulled. The bell joyfully announced to the entire countryside, "Hold on! Here we come!"

We gathered our books and papers and ran to the country store to wait for the buses. We lined up our books on the sidewalk to save our spots. Candy and Mike's daddy was the bus driver for the Four Buttes bus, and Candy was always the first one in line. Our bus wouldn't come for a while as we had to wait for the big bus to bring the older children from the school in Scobey.

We ran across the street to play in the ruins of the old grain elevator that had burned down years before. A new grain elevator was built and stood majestic across the way from the general store, but the basement walls from the old elevator were still there. We could climb down and play cops and robbers or cowboys and Indians. The children who hadn't brought their cap guns to school used pointed fingers or sticks for guns, and we played until Penny spied the bus coming to the store.

"The bus is here!" she yelled.

"I'm first," Candy reminded everyone as we climbed out of the basement ruins and ran to the bus to claim our seats.

Penny and Candy sat in the front seat, right behind the driver, Candy's daddy.

The big bus from Scobey came shortly afterwards, and the older children who lived south of Four Buttes transferred to our bus. We waited as they ran into the store to purchase their candy bars or to pick up the milk or bread their mothers had requested them to bring home.

Paul had a whole dollar, and spent all of it on penny pieces of Bazooka bubble gum. Paul didn't have enough time to count one hundred pieces of gum, so the storekeeper told Paul to take as many as he thought one hundred pieces would be. When he got home, he laid out his bubble gum and counted to see who got gypped, the store keeper or him. He had grabbed almost exactly one hundred pieces of gum.

It had been an exciting day. At the supper table we chattered about all that we had learned and all that we had done at school. Johnny told on me, how I had gotten in trouble for going to the restroom without permission, but Daddy winked and said, "Once you learn the rules you'll do just fine."

Four Buttes School

Chapter 3

After School

After we came home from school each afternoon I returned to my life of fun and make-believe. We were the only family I knew that had no television or indoor bathroom. Our house was made up of two homestead shanties. When the owners of the shanties married, they joined their homes as well as their hearts. They added a section on one side, and that was partitioned to make a small bedroom, a pantry, and a large closet. Daddy built an entry/mud room on the front of the house.

By the time I was born we had running water. Daddy had dug a full basement under the house and poured concrete for the floor and walls. The entry housed a ceramic sink, the cream separator, and an old wringer washing machine. Past the entry was the kitchen with Mom's electric range, refrigerator, cupboards and cabinets. Opposite the modern electric range stood the old coal cook stove which we used for heat in the winter. A homemade kitchen table with mismatched chairs was pushed against the wall.

The boys' bedroom, with a bunk bed and twin sized bed, was to the right of the kitchen. Boys' clothing was piled on the floor or hung on hangers in a small closet, and the drawers of the two paint chipped dressers were stuffed with the boys' pants and underwear. Johnny name was scratched across the top drawer with a pinwheel used for marking sewing patterns.

The walls in the boys' room had peeling wallpaper with a pattern of children on a carousal. The ceiling leaked like a sieve when it rained. The buckets and cans used to catch the rainwater that poured through the ceiling were stacked in the corner next to the training potty chair. With no indoor bathroom, the little potty chair was a matter of necessity. The path leading to the outhouse went around the feed granary and past the pig pen and chicken coop. It was dark and spooky late at night.

My sister's room was made out of the room that had served as the pantry. It was just large enough for her single bed, and one dresser. Daddy made a small closet for her to hang her modest wardrobe.

My parents slept on a foldout couch in the living room, and I still slept in the crib at the foot of their bed, next to the old oil stove.

The house was small, but we had miles of open prairie to roam and play. We had two border collie dogs, Tina, and Dixie, several barn cats, and two-house cats. There were chickens and pigs too. Most of the neighboring ranchers raised white-faced Herefords, but Daddy had black Angus beef cows. We had three milk cows, two Holsteins that came when we yelled, "Here Bossie, Bossie, Bossie, and a brown Guernsey named Rosie.

I loved the cats most of all. They were like babies, and I could dress them up in old baby clothes that I found stashed in boxes in the basement. Having three big brothers, I was a little embarrassed to play with dolls, so the animals were my baby dolls.

Buttons, the female house cat, and Zipper, the old toothless tomcat, didn't enjoy my games and went running when I came near. A neighbor gave us a cute black kitten, and I claimed it to be my very own. Inky wasn't as fond of me as I was of her. Although I held her, hugged her, dressed her, and slept with her, her sharp claws carved my arms, legs, face, and torso as she tried to maintain her dignity.

Some distance from the house was a big wooden shed with a cement floor, where Daddy parked the grain trucks when not in use. We called it "the big shed." Some afternoons we children went there to roller skate. We had enough roller skates for everyone. We could adjust their length and, with the roller skate key, we could also adjust them to fit any hard-soled shoes. I didn't like to skate as much as to ride my tricycle.

Johnny and I often joined the three older children in the big shed. David backed the grain trucks out, and we had to sweep the concrete floor clear of all the wheat and debris that could trip the skates.

Once, while the three older ones put their skates on, Johnny and I laid sticks down to make "train tracks" for a railroad crossing for our tricycles. When Carolyn, David and Paul had their skates adjusted and clamped on, they saw the "train tracks."

"We can't skate over train tracks," David argued. "Get rid of them right away."

Paul, who was closer to our age, understood our problem and appealed to us diplomatically. He figured out a way we could set up the "train tracks" so they would be out of the way of the skaters, and soon we were all going round and round on our respective wheels until it was time for chores.

The milk cows were often in the pasture just beyond the barnyard when it was milking time. I loved to go for the cows. Dixie, the dainty border-collie, followed Carolyn and me until we found the cows, usually at the far end of the pasture.

We called, "Heeeere Bossie, Bossie, Bossie! Heeeere Bossie, Bossie, Bossie!"

The cows, with their milk-bags so full of milk that they were nearly dragging on the ground, moseyed toward the barnyard as Dixie nipped at their heels. They entered the barn, each going to her own stall, and began eating the fresh grain and hay placed in the manger.

Milk and milk foam filled the pails as the boys squeezed out the warm milk. The faster the cow was milked, the more foam would form, and David and Paul raced to see who could make the most foam. Sometimes, when David or Paul pulled too hard while racing, the cow kicked the bucket; and they would lose a whole pail of milk.

Once in a while Paul let me help, but after a few squeezes I preferred to play in the hay shed, where Daddy's old saddle became my imaginary horse. I would ride the "wild broncos" until milking time was finished.

Paul playfully squirted milk off to the cats who sat a safe distance from the cows. "Here Kitty" he called as they quickly lapped up the milk in midair. After the cows had been sent back outside, David and Paul carefully filled the barn cats' dishes and left as the purring cats contentedly lapped up the warm milk.

Once in the house, David lifted the heavy pail of milk and carefully poured it into the cream separator. He and Paul took turns cranking the separator, and I watched as the cream trickled out one spout into a one-quart jar and the skim milk poured into a two-quart jar.

Sometimes Paul let me turn the crank as David replaced the full jars with empty jars. I had to be careful to crank fast enough, but not so fast that the skim milk went through the cream spout, as it would if they turned the crank too quickly. My arm grew weary quickly, and I was soon ready to let Paul resume his chore.

Once a week Mom emptied the refrigerator of all the unused cream that had accumulated. She placed a strainer over the top of the tall metal cream can and poured the cream, most of it sour, into the can. Daddy then took it to the Scobey train depot where it sat with numerous other cans full of sour cream until the train picked it up. It then continued its journey to an out-of-state creamery. Mom said it didn't matter if the cream was old.

I wrinkled my nose as Mom carefully stretched the screen cap over the top of the cream can, and began pouring in the thick lumpy cream. "Why are you pouring that rotten cream in the cream can?" I asked.

"It's not rotten," Mom explained. "It's old, and some is a bit soured. The creamery can process it so you'd never know it's old. The stores in town buy butter and ice cream from a creamery that uses this kind of cream."

I never thought of that sour cream when I ate store-bought ice cream. The creamery did a good job of turning that sour cream into my favorite summertime dessert.

After the supper dishes were washed it was time to get ready for school the next day. Carolyn, David, and Paul sat at the kitchen table and worked on their homework. Daddy sat in the corner and read a book or studied his Bible for his Sunday school class next week. Johnny and I played together until Mom was ready for story time.

Paul, Johnny, and I snuggled with her on the old green couch as we decided what story she would tell. Sometimes she read Bible stories, sometimes an old fairy tale. Even better than that, she sometimes told us stories in which we were the characters. She included our toys and our friends when she made up stories.

"Once upon a time," she began, "in a little prairie house, lived a little girl and two little boys.

Johnny and I giggled. We knew Johnny and Paul were the little boys and I was the little girl.

"The little girl loved her big brothers, and followed them everywhere. They were allowed to explore the big farm with all the sheds and machinery. Nearby lived a neighbor. The little boys and the little girl did not know the neighbor, but all the children at school said the neighbor was a giant, and a very angry giant.

One day the children ran along the lane near the neighbor's house. They were chasing butterflies and picking bluebells and buttercups to grace their mother's table. The biggest boy, Paul, tripped and fell and hurt his knee. He couldn't get up. The little girl asked, 'What should we do?'

"'I don't know!" Paul cried, 'but I need help.'

"Johnny said, 'We need to go ask the giant for help. But I'm scared.'"

"I'm scared too," said Kathy, "Let's go together."

Kathy and Johnny ran as fast as they could to the giant's house and stood before the great big door. Kathy was scared, but she knew she must ask for help. Johnny cautiously approached the door, knocked on the door, then ran to the end of the walk.

Slowly the door creaked opened, and a very tall man asked gruffly, 'Who knocked on my door?'

"'We did,' answered the little boy, as his voice quivered. 'We're your neighbors, and our brother has hurt his knee. Please can you help us?'"

The man looked at the children, and looked to the left and to the right. 'I don't see a boy. Where is he?'"

"'We will take you to him,' they said.

"The little girl suddenly realized something. This man sat alone in church every Sunday morning. He was a sad man. He had no children, and people said his wife was very ill.

"When they reached the little boy, the giant examined his leg carefully. 'I think you twisted your leg.' he said. 'I will carry you to your house.'"

"He picked the little boy up in his big, strong arms, and the little girl led the way to their home.

"You are a kind man,' the Johnny said. 'What is your name?'"

"'I am Brownie,' he replied."

Johnny and I giggled. That was the name of Daddy's old horse.

"From that day on, the little boy and the little girl played all over the farm, but once a week they picked flowers and ran to Brownie's house to give flowers to his wife and visit with him."

We knew it was time to go to bed when Mom finished the story. As Mom tucked us into our beds and kissed us, we slipped into dreamland, secure in the knowledge that we were the most important people in the whole world.

Story Time

Chapter 4

Holiday Time

As the days grew shorter the skies became grey and dreary. We no longer looked forward to recess time. Recess was the teacher's break, so she would scoot us out so we "could get some fresh air," and she could relax with her cup of coffee.

All the girls in the big school in Scobey had to wear dresses every day. Our teacher allowed us to wear pants. We still wore dresses to school two or three times a week, but once the temperatures began to plummet, we wore slacks under our dresses.

Daddy and Grandpa brought home the beef cows that had been out in the distant pasture, in preparation for the approaching winter. Last year Daddy had built a large three-sided shed out of planks of lumber as shelter for the cows. The winds came mostly from the north and northwest, so he built the shed with an open southern exposure. Each evening he pitched loose hay from the haystack into the mangers and carried pitchforks of straw to the shed for bedding for the cattle.

He and the boys cared for the milk cows in the barn. As David and Paul squirted the warm milk into the buckets the cold air caused steam to rise from the pails. The cats, wearing thick coats of fur, huddled together waiting for their warm meal of milk.

Our house was poorly insulated and drafty, but our two stoves helped keep out the late autumn chill. Daddy kept the cook stove in the kitchen hot with the coal he carried in from the nearby coal shed. The oil stove in the living room provided additional warmth.

I loved to sit on the floor next to the cozy fire with our blue portable record player on days that were too cold to play outside, and listen to my favorite 45 speed records with nursery songs. My favorite record featured Burl Ives as he sang, "There's a little white duck, sittin' on the wata', a little white duck, doin' what he otta." Johnny liked listening to "Peter and the Wolf," but that was too scary for me. We had story records and children's music that kept me happy for hours.

Listening to the Old Radio

The old radio stood tall and majestic, and sometimes a lady read stories. I enjoyed getting lost in the stories. I wondered how she could possibly fit in our radio. I didn't understand it, but assumed she must be very little.

We were learning many new things in school. During story time Mrs. Trang read to us about the Pilgrims and the Mayflower. She prepared the sixth graders for the report they were to write about the Mayflower. She gave the fourth and fifth graders information for the page they would write about the first Thanksgiving. The third graders would be writing a paragraph about the Pilgrims, and she explained to them the importance of supporting the topic sentence with the other statements in the paragraph. Then she went to the metal cabinet where games, flash cards, and art supplies were stored. She brought out the colored modeling clay. We first graders were to use it to recreate the first Thanksgiving feast.

We were each assigned to make a specific item for the feast. Kristi was to make the turkey. Ellen was to make the bread and vegetables. My job was to make the dinner plates.

At first the clay was hard, but as we worked it the warmth from our hands made it more pliable and before long it was quite sticky.

Kristi was intent on getting the turkey legs to stick up just like they did at her house on Thanksgiving Day. Elinor worked on the pies, and Mike and Ray worked on the deer that was to roast over the open fire. I quickly made the plates out of the brown clay. They looked drab, so I rolled little balls of red and yellow clay back and forth until they looked like little worms. I attached them to the plates and added a green clay rim to hide where the tentacles were attached. Then I squeezed tiny balls of the colored clay to make polka-dots on the platters.

After Kristi finished her turkey, she rolled a string of clay and squeezed it to her ear lobe.

"Look at my earrings!" she said.

We laughed. Elinor made a necklace out of the green clay. Ellen made a bracelet and Mike made handcuffs. I made a pair of earrings out of yellow and red clay twisted together. The warm gooey clay wouldn't stay on my ear lobes, so I stuck it into my ear. Soon we were all sticking the clay into our ears, up our noses, and around our necks.

Mrs. Trang was busy in the library, helping the older girls find more information on the Mayflower. When she came out of the library, we hurriedly removed the jewelry and handcuffs. She glared at us in disbelief. We knew we had crossed the line. She peeled the tentacles off my beautiful plates and exclaimed, "That looks nothing like the plates the Pilgrims used!"

Then she saw what Kristi and I had done to our ears. "What the world! What did you do?" she ranted.

She dismissed the other students for recess, but Kristi and I had to stay inside. She first worked on Kristi's ears, trying to get all the warm clay out. Kristi hadn't stuffed it in quite as far as I had and was soon able to go out to play.

Mrs. Trang grumbled the whole time she worked on my ears. "Why would you do such a thing? Don't you know any better? What made you think you should do this? Pilgrims didn't wear jewelry. I can't believe you did this! It goes in farther than I can reach with this Q-tip! What will your mother say?"

She muttered and muttered, but she didn't want me to answer. Eventually she did manage to complete the job, and sent me out with the rest of the children so she could get some aspirin and gain her composure before calling us back in.

One day Mike said, "I got a really funny joke."

"Mike!" scolded Candy. "You're not supposed to tell that joke."

Mike walked away from the older girls. The first graders followed him.

"Come on, tell us the joke," Ellen urged.

"Not with Kathy here, though," Elinor said.

"Yeah, Kathy's too young. You'd better go away, cause you're still a baby," Kristi agreed.

"I'm just a few months younger than you, Kristi," I blurted in my defense.

"Well, when you turn six, then we'll be able to let you hear dirty jokes, but until then you had better go away," she insisted.

They stood around Mike, silent until I walked away.

"They won't let me play with them because they say I'm a baby," I cried to Mrs. Trang. I didn't dare tell her they were telling dirty jokes.

Mrs. Trang wasn't fond of the fact that I was allowed to come to school so young. "Maybe you should just bring a doll and play in the corner away from the rest of the kids," she snapped.

"Oh, okay," I chirped. "I have a doll that bends at its elbows and closes its eyes when you lay it down to sleep."

"Yes," she said more softly, thinking I hadn't noticed her harsh tone before. "That would be a good idea."

That night as we sat at the supper table, I told Mom and Daddy, "Mrs. Trang told me I could bring a doll in to school and play in the corner away from the rest of the kids because they all think I'm a baby."

Daddy knew Mrs. Trang was reluctant to have me in school. "She what? No, you are in school, and your friends are in your class. You go to school and play with your friends. What do you suppose she was thinking?" Daddy looked at Mom. I knew he was going to have a talk with Mrs. Trang when I saw that look. I knew better than to tell him my classmates wouldn't let me hear their "dirty jokes."

We were learning to read. We finished The Red Book and were beginning the next primers. Tom, Betty and Susan, the characters in the readers, were becoming our friends. I loved the paper-covered primers, but I could hardly wait to get to the big hard-covered reader, "The Little White House." It looked more like Johnny's reader.

We enjoyed reading about Flip, the dog, and Bunny, Susan's stuffed animal. One of the first days we started reading I memorized everything we read.

Barbee, Kristi's mom, came to visit the school one day, and I was eager to show her how well I read. I opened the little red primer and recited, "Tom. Ride Tom, ride."

She teased, "You can't read. You just memorized that."

She expected me to defend myself and convince her that I really could read, but she was right. I wondered how she knew!

Christmas was coming, and it was time to prepare for the school Christmas program. The first graders had to continue with Pasting Pages and school lessons. The other children worked on their recitations, their musical numbers, and the two plays that would be presented for the community the evening of the program.

The teacher had a special little play for the first graders. In the play we stood around a suitcase on the homemade stage and contemplated what could be in the mysterious bag. We each had to memorize our lines. I practiced my part over and over. With as much expression as I could display, I warned, "It might be bears, even bugs! Let's run away and hide!"

We decorated the entire school with handmade art projects. Bows, cutouts, and paper snowflakes adorned the walls and windows. The fragrance of the tall decorated Christmas tree filled the room.

The teacher helped each of us make a spray-painted hand print in plaster for our parents. We wrapped them carefully in colorful paper and placed them under the tree, to be presented to our parents by Santa Claus the night of the play.

The night of the production came at last, and we dressed in our Christmas finery—new dresses and patent leather shoes for the girls, and new pants and shirts for the boys. Candy and Mike always had the nicest clothes. I thought Candy was the prettiest girl I had ever seen. She was Mary, and we first-graders were the angels in the nativity scene.

Nativity Scene

An appreciative audience of parents, grandparents, aunts and uncles and neighbors sitting on make-shift benches crowded the school room.

We bowed to loud applause as the final curtain closed. Santa Claus rushed in with his jolly "Ho, ho, ho," as we sang "Here comes Santa Claus, here comes Santa Claus, right down Santa Claus Lane..."

He gave each girl and boy the gifts that Mrs. Trang had supplied, and then gave everyone a red net stocking full of hard Christmas candy, chocolate truffles, fruit and nuts. We had each drawn the name of a classmate to be given a gift, and these, too, were distributed, along with big, red delicious apples donated by the grain elevator.

Neighbors congratulated the neighbors' children on their excellent performances. Someone stepped on my plaster hand print and cracked it into two pieces, but Daddy assured me he could glue it and it would be as good as new.

Christmas vacation was finally here, and it would soon be Christmas eve. Secrets were being whispered, and one room in the basement was kept locked. Occasionally I heard the trap door in the kitchen ceiling open and shut in the night as Daddy hid some treasure in the attic in preparation for the big night. Mom spent hours in the kitchen baking special cut-out sugar cookies, molded cookies, fruitcake, and our favorite pies.

Two days before Christmas Mom got the whole family together to make lefsa. Lefsa was from Daddy's Norwegian background, and it was just as necessary as the slippery Norwegian-prepared cod fish known as "lutefisk" for Christmas Eve.

The older children peeled and cut up twenty pounds of potatoes. As soon as they were cooked, Mom mashed them with her big mixer, adding milk, butter and salt. Then she added flour and rolled the dough into large flat thin disks, big enough to cover the top of the special, round electric lefsa griddle. Daddy helped the boys roll the flat dough carefully around a round wooden stick, and then unroll it onto the hot surface of the griddle. As bubbles formed in the dough, they used a long, flat wooden stick to turn it to bake the other side. To eat the spotted "potato tortilla" we spread it with butter and a generous sprinkling of brown or white sugar, and rolled it like a jelly roll. We ate it as a bread with special holiday meals, but we ate a good share of it warm from the griddle.

Christmas Eve came. The presents under the tree were begging to be opened. Mom and Daddy worked together in the kitchen preparing the traditional meal of lutefisk and oyster stew. Since we children didn't like lutefisk or oyster stew, Mom also prepared fried chicken, mashed potatoes and gravy. Grandpa and our widowed neighbor, Mr. Miller, joined us for the feast.

The meal wasn't the important event for us children. We had to eat and get all the dishes washed and put away before Santa Claus could come. This was one meal Mom and Daddy didn't lift a finger to help in the clean-up. It was up to us.

As the final dish was washed and put away, we urged Mom and Daddy to start with the traditional ritual. They sent us to the boys' bedroom with strict instructions not to peek.

Santa Claus was going to make a quick appearance, just to deliver a few things. We heard the door downstairs open. We heard the trap door in the kitchen ceiling open. We heard Santa as he laughed a hearty "ho-ho-ho" in a voice that sounded surprisingly like our own Daddy's.

Then we heard a faint jingle of sleigh bells, and we guessed Santa must be ready to leave.

"I don't hear anything!" I exclaimed. "It's quiet! Santa must have left!"

David peeked through the skeleton key hole in the door. "I can't see anything. It's dark."

"David!" Carolyn scolded. "You can't peek!"

"Yeah! What if Santa catches you," I said.

After what seemed to be an eternity, Mom called for us to come. The kitchen was dark. Daddy had turned off the lights. As we entered the living room, the twinkling Christmas tree lights reflected from the lead tinsel icicles and glass ball decorations on the tree's branches and shone on beautifully wrapped presents underneath. I heard Daddy tell Mr. Miller harvest had been good this year, although I didn't understand what difference that would make when it came to Santa's generosity.

In front of the tree sat a brand-new child-sized folding table with four matching chairs, just my size. David and Paul gingerly picked up the new .22 caliber rifles that Santa had decorated with a large red bow. Mom had bought me a two-foot-high doll that kind of walked as I held its hand, and each of us exclaimed our excitement as we opened our gifts.

Then Daddy brought out a big box with more presents. Uncle Homer, Daddy's bachelor brother, had no children of his own, and found great pleasure in buying gifts for his nephews and nieces. Nobody else in the world understood what would bring pleasure to a child more than my Uncle Homer. This year I received a toy doggie that barked and jumped when I pushed the buttons on the attached cord.

Soon it was bedtime. After we carefully hung our net stockings on our bed posts, or crib posts, we snuggled in our beds, and reluctantly fell asleep so Santa could return. When we awakened in the morning, we found our stockings stuffed with candy, fruit, and more presents. There were pocket knives for David and Paul, watercolors for me, a new watch for Carolyn and a flashlight for Johnny.

Grandpa, Mr. Miller, and the new intern who helped the pastor at our Lutheran church, joined us for Christmas Dinner. Christmas Dinner was a formal dinner where we sat around the big oak table and used our manners as we feasted on turkey and all the trimmings. This time Mom set the new little card table up for Johnny and me and we dined in our private corner.

We spent the rest of the day playing with our new toys, visiting with the grownups, and playing board games.

I enjoyed Christmas vacation but I could hardly wait to get back to school to show my friends all my neat toys.

The end of Christmas vacation finally came, but instead of returning to school, I lay in my crib with a high fever. Mumps was a common childhood disease in those days, and I had to be isolated for over a week.

The days dragged on until, finally, I felt better. I found Mom in the kitchen making an angel food cake. Angel food cake was the official birthday cake in our house. We thought it was the tastiest of desserts. It was January eighth, and Mom told me today was my birthday. I was finally six years old!

I knew I would never have a little brother or sister now. I was six and, although I wasn't sure, I reasoned that, since I didn't know anyone with children six years apart, Mom probably couldn't have any more children. I decided I'd best stop pestering Mom for a baby.

Kristi's mom stopped over and gave me a red plastic purse filled with toy jewelry and a hair brush, and congratulated me on becoming such a big girl. I was finally the same age as Kristi, and nobody could tease me about being the baby ever again.

Chapter 5

The Lumpy Loaf

Whenever I begin to bake
My daughter spends an hour
Helping Mom to mix and knead
The sugar, yeast, and flour.

She sets her dab of dough to raise
And forms a loaf like mine,
Although the shape turns out to be
Of weird and strange design.

She does not care that flour paste
Besmears her hair and dress.
Her eagerness ignores the fact
The kitchen is a mess.

The little loaf, the lumpy loaf
Is baked and browned just so,
And Kathy is the proudest cook,
Whoever kneaded dough!

By Dorothy Rustebakke

My mom was a newspaper reporter. She wasn't the business-suit kind with a paper badge marked PRESS tucked in the band of a small-brimmed business hat. That kind works for the daily newspapers in big cities like Billings or Great Falls. She was more the windblown-hair, camera-hanging-around-her-neck-type, with an over-sized purse containing another camera, flash attachment, film, a stenographer's notebook and a couple of pencils. This kind works at a small-town weekly newspaper office.

Mom's Typewriter

One day, while walking down the sidewalk, we came upon two ladies deep in conversation. As we approached them from behind, I heard one lady say, "I think Dorothy Rustebakke is a wonderful writer. She brings everything to life. What an asset to the local paper." The other lady whole heartedly agreed, and when they realized my mother probably heard their comments they blushed and greeted her politely as we passed by.

"Mom!" I declared indignantly. "They were talking about you!"

My mother just smiled at me, and when we were down the street a bit she simply said, "The only thing worse than being talked about is not being talked about."

One day Mom said, "I'm going to Maurice Murphy's place to interview Janice and Gary." Gary and Janice were rodeo champions. Gary had won the National High School Bulldogging title last year and was now competing in college rodeos. He was the all-around cowboy in several rodeos and was doing very well in his rodeo adventures. At the Wolf Point Stampede, he had bulldogged a steer in 3.3 seconds. Janice competed in barrel racing, pole bending and cow cutting and had won the all-around cowgirl title two years in a row in District 1, and was also a rodeo queen. Joslyn, their younger sister, was nine years old. Candy, Michael, and Connie were their cousins.

"Can I go with you?" I asked.

"I think that will be all right," Mom replied.

The Murphy ranch was just two miles west of our place. A cattle guard in the form of a metal grate lay across the entrance to their driveway, which was framed with an arch centered with their "Rocking M" brand. The Murphy family were ranchers more than farmers, and I loved the western-style house they lived in.

Candy was visiting her cousin, Joslyn. As Mom visited with Janice and Gary, jotting notes in squiggly shorthand characters, Joslyn said, "Let's go downstairs and play school."

Candy and I followed her obediently downstairs.

Gary's bedroom was in the basement. The tan wall in his room was decorated with black brands, and looked wonderfully "western." Beautiful saddles were stacked on top of each other.

"Where did all these saddles come from?" I asked Joslyn.

"Some are Janice's and some are Gary's. They are trophy saddles they won at high school rodeos. Janice is a barrel racer. That's why your mom is interviewing her. She just won this saddle." She showed me the newest addition to the collection.

"What does a barrel racer do?" I asked.

"She races her horse around barrels. The fastest horse wins."

I didn't know what barrel racing was. I imagined the horses all running at the same time in circles around barrels. I wondered how they decided when to start and when to end.

Joslyn had part of the basement set up like a school room. She had two desks and a chalkboard was mounted on the wall. She had old papers from school that were our pretend homework papers. Some of the papers had good grades, but some had failing grades Joslyn explained her rules.

"I'm the teacher, Candy is the smart student and you are the dumb one," she said to me.

She stood at the chalkboard with a piece of real chalk in her hand.

"Okay students, I want you to come to the board and answer these problems. These are yours, Candy."

She jotted down some addition problems for Candy. $4 + 2$, $3 + 6$, and $1 + 5$.

"These are yours, Kathy." She wrote $259 + 38$. I didn't know how to add big numbers. I was in first grade. Mrs. Trang had only taught me how to add and subtract little numbers.

Candy answered her problems quickly. "Very good Candy! You are so smart. I'm proud of you. Okay, Kathy, now you do your problems."

"I don't know how."

"What do you mean?"

"I never learned this," I said in my defense.

"I taught you this last week! Don't you remember? You need to try!" she demanded.

I wrote "6" under the sum line.

"Wrong! You will have to study much harder" she said in her "teacher" voice.

Tears began to well in my eyes.

"Joslyn, don't be so mean to her," Candy protested.

"Fine," Joslyn said. "Sit at that desk." She pointed to the oldest, most scratched desk of all. Joslyn's name was scratched deep on the wooden top of the desk.

"Here are your homework papers. Candy, you did very well. All 'A's," she said as she paged through the stack of papers, giving her the best ones.

"Kathy, you must study harder. I might have to flunk you." She handed me several homework sheets with bold red "Fs" slashed angrily across them. They were Joslyn's real homework papers.

"Did you really get 'F's?" I asked.

"No–they are all 'A's", I just erased the side and made it into an "F", so we could play school with the papers," she snapped. "Now Kathy, I want you to write, 'I will study harder for my next test' five times."

I started writing, but a lump formed in my throat and tears welled in my eyes. "I'm going to find Mom," I managed to say.

Joslyn knew she would be in trouble. "No, no," she pleaded. "Let's not play school any more. Do you want to see the horses?"

Maybe Joslyn would be nicer if we did something else. I loved horses more than anything else, so I followed her eagerly up the stairs.

I heard Mom in the kitchen ask Janice, "Do you think your little sister will follow in your footsteps?"

Janice laughed. "Joslyn isn't quite like me in my love for horses. We can hardly get her on a horse. She probably won't do much with high school rodeos."

Joslyn ushered us out the side door so my mom wouldn't see us.

"Wait here for a minute," Joslyn said as she ran back into the house.

"Don't mind Joslyn," Candy whispered. "She can be a lot of fun. She likes to be bossy, but you don't have to let her."

Joslyn came out of the house wearing her cowboy shirt and cowboy boots. I thought she looked really pretty dressed like that. We followed her to the barn where her horse was stabled.

Janice and Gary came out of the house and posed for pictures as Mom looked through the top of her twin-lens reflex camera. Janice's hair was braided in a long single braid down her back.

"I probably look bald," Janice laughed, adjusting her cowboy hat. She brought her long braid in front. "There. At least people can tell I have hair."

Joslyn let me get on her horse. I decided then that she was nice. I thought there would be nothing more exciting that to belong to a family like that. They were real cowboys.

It was time to go.

"Joslyn was mean today before we went outside," I told Mom on the way home.

"She's having a hard time," Mom said to excuse her actions. "Her Mom is very ill and may have to go to Seattle to be on a kidney machine just to stay alive."

I had heard that Mrs. Murphy was sick, but I didn't realize how serious it was.

I was proud of my mother, but she occasionally did things that just weren't appreciated by little girls. Once in a while she would write something about one of us children. When her poem, "The Lumpy Loaf", was published, Mr. Eide, a kind older gentleman, leaned through the window in the car and pinched my cheek.

"Is this the Lumpy Loaf?" he asked.

She laughed and said, "Yes, that's our little baker."

As well as being a newspaper reporter and writer, Mom was a wonderful cook and made delicious baked goods. I enjoyed being with her when she was interviewing someone for an article, but Johnny and I liked working in the kitchen with her even more. Bread baking day was a special time.

She brought out the big stainless-steel dish pan that she used only for making bread. She measured several cups of warm water, testing the temperature with her wrist like someone testing a baby's bath water. The temperature had to be just right so the yeast would work. Then she added the sugar, shortening, salt, yeast, and finally the flour. As she mixed and added more flour, the dough finally became thick enough to work by hand. When she could form it into a lump, she dumped it onto the floured table, and we kneaded it over and over again. I loved the feeling of the lump of warm dough. It reminded me of a fat belly.

Johnny and I punched it with our fists as Mom leaned into the dough with the palms of her hands. Over and over, we worked more flour into the dough, until finally it was ready to raise.

Mom cleaned out the large stainless-steel tub of all the loose flour and dough, greased it, and put the smooth round lump of yeast dough back in the tub. Then she covered it with a damp tea towel and let it rise.

After an hour the dough was ready to work again. She rolled the lump again onto the floury table, and sliced the huge mass into ten sections. After she formed each section into a smooth ball, she left the dough on the table to "rest." As the dough "rested" beside the warm coal cook stove, she heated the electric oven and we greased nine pans. Then she gave Johnny and me each a little loaf pan to grease.

Having attractive, smooth loaves of bread was important to Mom. When the balls of dough were ready to form into loaves, she cut one in half and gave Johnny and me our own lumps of dough to form into our very own loaves of bread. We shaped and worked the dough so it would fit just right in our little loaf pans. No matter how hard we tried to form our dough like Mom's large loaves, we each created our own lumpy loaf. Mine was always the lumpiest.

Once again Mom placed the pans of bread on the table to raise. After the loaves had doubled in size, she put them into the heated oven to bake. When they were done, she pulled them out, steaming hot and golden brown. Only the smell of fresh baked cookies compared in my mind to the aroma of freshly baked bread.

We waited for the bread to cool off just enough so it could be sliced. Fresh creamy butter and homemade chokecherry jelly made the hot bread a snack that was good enough to serve to the president of the United States. The president was, to us, the most important man in the world, and he was the standard to measure just how good or important something was. If it were good enough for him, it was good enough for anybody.

Mom removed the rest of the loaves from the pans and set them on the cooling racks on the table. Then she washed the baking dishes and cleaned the kitchen. Johnny and I wrapped our hot loaves in tea towels and went to his bedroom. We sat on the top bunk bed, each with our own lumpy loaf, waiting for them to cool.

"I can make my own bed," Johnny confided in me.

"You didn't make it today. It's a mess."

"I'll show you."

I went to the corner of the bed, holding both loaves so he could work. He tucked the sheets in and pulled the blankets smoothly over the mattress. He tucked the bedspread under the pillow, and over top to make a smooth hump just like Kristi's mom did to their beds. He did a good job!

Then he pulled the blankets down and untucked the sheets and crumpled the bed covers up.

"Don't tell Mom I can make my bed," he warned.

"Why not? She'd be happy!"

"Yeah, but if she knows I can make my own bed, then she'll make me do it every day!"

We each broke open our lumpy loaf, and the steam was warm and fragrant. We weren't fond of the crust. Like the middle of a watermelon, the center of the loaf was the best. As we chatted, we pinched off pieces of warm white bread and enjoyed the tasty manna. By the time we were done only the lumpy shell was left.

Mom wasn't happy with us when she saw what we had done, and she scolded us.

Daddy laughed when she told him, and he gently reminded her that we did make them, and they were our loaves. Nevertheless, we knew we shouldn't do that again.

Helping Mom Bake

Chapter 6
Church

We were the only children around that didn't have an indoor bathroom. Mom's parents had lived in the state of Washington. They raised Mom in Tacoma where she had indoor plumbing, electric lights, and an indoor bathroom since childhood. She married my father, a tall, handsome soldier that she had met during World War II. Dazzled by his charm, she followed him back in time to this rural corner of Montana.

Since they moved to this homestead shanty, they had made many improvements. They now had electricity. An electric pump replaced the hand water pump. They had hot and cold water now, and telephone service reached our isolated home, but we still had to journey past the feed granary, pig pen and chicken coop to the old outhouse whenever nature called.

The rinse tub Mom used for rinsing the clothes when she used the wringer washing machine became my bathtub Saturday afternoons. Daddy took the galvanized steel tub off the heavy nail in the entry and put it on the kitchen table. Mom put in enough warm water so I could play, and for over an hour I splashed and imagined I was far out to sea. When I had splashed most of the water from the tub, Mom finally said it was time to wash my hair. I squeezed my eyes shut as tightly as I could, but soap almost always got into my eyes. She rinsed my hair until no shampoo residue was left. She knew my hair was clean when she rubbed it with her fingers and it squeaked.

Bath Time

My fine blond hair was unruly, full of static electricity in this dry climate, so Mom discovered the perfect remedy; a rinse that was supposed to calm the wildest hair. She mixed a capful of the miracle product with a cup of water and poured it carefully over my hair. The smell was pungent, and no matter how hard I cried, Mom insisted on the procedure and worked the solution into my hair. The solution stung my eyes, and, after waiting two minutes, she finally rinsed the smelly stuff from my hair. She wrapped me in a stiff, fresh wind-dried towel that relaxed and softened as it surrounded my wet, shivering body. I cuddled with her. I was six, but I still liked her to play "This little piggy went to market" on my toes.

After I dressed, she wrapped small locks of my short damp hair around her finger and crisscrossed bobby pins so my hair would be curly for church tomorrow. After Daddy dumped my bath water, he again filled the small tub for Johnny. Daddy then brought the large galvanized bathtub up from the basement and drew warm water for each boy and Carolyn. One by one they bathed and warmed themselves, wrapped with towels, by the hot oil-stove. Daddy drew fresh water for the next, until we were all squeaky clean for Sunday school and church.

"It's time to get up boys," Daddy called.

"We have to get the morning chores done before church!"

David and Paul quickly pulled on their long johns and jeans and dressed in their heavy farm coats. The cows had to be milked, the dogs and cats fed, and the Angus herd had to be fed and bedded.

Mom tended the waffle iron as she prepared our favorite Sunday breakfast.

"Carolyn, please help Johnny and Kathy get ready."

Carolyn helped Johnny and me dress in our special Sunday clothes. I could pull my own long stockings up, once she helped me get them started with the heel in the right place, but I needed help clasping the garters that held them up. I put on my new slip and chose my favorite red wool dress, made for me by Mrs. Nielson, a childless Christian friend who loved to sew for little girls. Carolyn took the bobby pins from my hair, and I shook my head so the curls bounced as she brushed through my short curls.

I sat down to eat breakfast with an apron tied around my neck to protected my beautiful Sunday clothes. Mom set my hot waffle before me, and Carolyn buttered it and poured the homemade chokecherry syrup, careful to fill each square in the waffle.

Once the chores were done, Daddy and the boys ate quickly and dressed in their handsome suits and neckties. As they tied their freshly polished church shoes, Daddy realized his Sunday school book was missing. Mom finally found it on the large old radio that stood in the corner of the living room, under a pile of books and papers. Off we scrambled, putting on coats, boots and mittens before we piled into the car.

Before we got in the car Daddy knelt by me and said, "Honey, you're getting to be a big girl."

I swelled with pride that Daddy noticed.

"You need to stop sitting on your mother's lap during church service. It's hard for her to concentrate on the sermon when you wiggle and try to sleep on her lap. Church only lasts for an hour. Do you think you can sit on the pew without having to sit on Mommy's lap?"

I nodded, with a self-determination that I was now a big girl.

Daddy always aimed to get to the early service. The 9:00 a.m. service only lasted an hour because Sunday school started at ten. There were no restraints, no guarantees that the eleven o'clock service would be over by noon, and once it's that late half the day has gone by!

As we pulled up to the church, I saw my grandfather's car parked a block away, just past the fire hall. Grandpa was always the first person at church, but he never took one of the close parking spots.

As Daddy parked our creamy-white Chevy station wagon, Kristi's dad parked their red station wagon. Daddy greeted him and said, "I know we're late now. The Shipsteads are here."

Barbee, Kristi's mom, laughed and said, "That's just what Jim said! We know we're late. The Rustebakkes are here."

The bell in the steeple tolled as we entered the foyer. The ushers led us past all the congregation as they stood to sing the first hymn. We took our places and found the page in the hymnal that was being sung. Lutherans are known for sitting in the back of the church, and the early bird got the back pews. We were late, and only the first two rows of seats had enough room for all of us.

Sitting quietly for a whole hour was hard for me. Johnny and I tried to sing along with the hymns, but I didn't know the words to any of them. Mom told me when I was little, holding my hymnal upside-down, I sang at the top of my lungs, "Teeter-totter, bread and butter, wash your hands in dirty water." I thought that was funny. Apparently, everyone else did too.

After a couple hymns and the responsive readings printed out in the bulletin, the preacher climbed the steps to his pulpit and, from his high pinnacle, began with a scripture reading. Dressed in a white floor-length preacher's gown, he looked majestic, somewhat like God. He started talking in a quiet, commanding voice, but half way through the message he seemed to get angry and started shaking his finger and waving his arms. Although I didn't understand what he was talking about, I was sure he wasn't happy with little girls that wiggled too much, so I climbed on my mother's lap and buried my face until he was done with his sermon.

After the sermon, just like it said in the bulletin, it was time for the offering. I thought people would pay him more if he got their money before he yelled at them. The gold-rimmed offering plate came to me. I had to get sole custody of the plate before I would deposit my pennies. Then I passed it to my brother.

After church, we went to the basement where our Sunday school classes met. Barbee Shipstead was my teacher. Kristi and I sat next to each other. Barbee had three little girls and only two boys. She was ladylike, and she helped me remember to sit properly, like a little lady. She was careful to let me know if my slip was showing.

We punched out our paper cutouts and listened to the stories and ate our snack of black Hydrox sandwich cookies and red Kool-Aid. Mom never allowed me to have Kool-Aid and cookies in the morning except Sunday mornings at church.

When Sunday school was over, I went upstairs to the church office. Daddy was there getting the reel-to-reel tape recorder. He always recorded the Sunday morning message. Before leaving town, he took the large recording machine along with the reel to Grandma Brenden. She was a sweet older lady who was unable to go to church. Daddy set up the tape recorder and turned it on so she could worship along with the tape.

We stopped at the post office to pick up the mail. Although the post office window bars were down and no over-the-counter business was done on Sunday, the postmaster was behind the wall whistling as he deposited mail into the pigeon hole mail boxes. Daddy came out with the mail wrapped in the two Sunday papers and commented, "Well, the bird's in his cage again."

On the drive home Mom and the older children took apart The Billings Gazette and The Great Falls Tribune and distributed it to everyone according to his interests. Mom liked reading Ann Landers and Dear Abby. Of course, she checked over any feature article that she may have submitted. The rest of us shared the comic section, and if something was particularly funny someone read it out loud. Daddy, who was driving, was more interested in the news, and said the intelligence of people was displayed by the section of the newspaper they turned to. To him, our choices of Ann Landers and the Comics were at the bottom of the barrel.

On Monday morning Daddy went back to town to take the tape recorder to the next shut-in. Then he stopped at the church and picked up the bags containing the Sunday offering. It was his job as the elected church financial secretary to count the money, record everyone's contributions, and deposit the money in the bank.

Daddy cleared off the old, round oak table and counted the money there. Sometimes people deposited their contributions in offering envelopes without writing the amount on the outside. Daddy had to count the money, mark the envelopes, and record the contributions for tax purposes.

When I was 4-years-old, I knew it took money to buy candy from the little general store in Four Buttes. Daddy was clear that we were not to touch the money on the table. I wasn't in school yet. When Daddy went out to do the noon chores one day, he left the entire table covered with shiny coins and crisp paper bills. I thought of all the candy I could buy. I opened all the envelopes and carefully gathered all the pennies and other coins and put them in a jar. I knew how to spend the paper money with a "one" on it, but the bigger bills were unfamiliar to me. I separated the dollar bills from the larger denominations. I stuffed the ones I knew how to spend under the sofa cushions, in the blankets of my crib, between books in the bookcase, and under the clothes in the closet in the boys' room. I gathered all the larger bills and hid them in various nooks and crannies. I gathered the checks and put them in an empty oatmeal box that I hid in the crowded closet next to the living room. Then I went outside to play in the sand.

It wasn't long before Daddy came in the house and discovered his missing treasure. He ran outside and exclaimed, "Kathy! What did you do?"

Totally unaware of my "sin," I didn't understand what he was referring to until I saw the empty offering envelopes in his hands. There was no fibbing; there were no clever words; there was nothing I could do but plead for his mercy.

After a spanking I was sure I was forgiven. Daddy held me, and dried my tears, and assured me he still loved me. I hopped off his knee, totally reformed, vowing I would never do that again, and started for the door to go back to the sand hole.

"Not so fast, young lady," Daddy said. "Where's the money?"

I had no idea. I found most of the dollar bills and the coins. That was all I was interested in, anyhow.

For the next two weeks I was "grounded," until I found every five-, ten-, and twenty-dollar bill and every check that had been on the table.

Daddy had to go over all the offering envelopes and guess how much money each person had donated that week. Some people kept careful records and would compare their records against the church's records at the end of the year. For weeks another dollar or five turned up in the most unexpected places.

I don't know if Daddy ever told people about this terrible deed. I certainly didn't brag about it. Nevertheless, I was so ashamed that I hid behind Daddy every time I saw my Sunday school teacher from that year. I was sure God told the pastor what a naughty girl I was. And for years I pondered how a little girl with such a nice mommy and daddy could have stolen the entire church offering.

Chapter 7
Springtime

I was growing tired of the long winter days. The weather was so cold that we had to bundle up in layers of thermal underwear, stretch pants, snow suits, and knitted scarves and hats. At the beginning of the winter, we each had new mittens and gloves but now every time we went to play, we no longer expected to find a matching pair. We stirred around the box of mittens and gloves, hoping to find one that fit the left hand and one that fit the right hand.

The cows started calving in the early spring, and this was a busy time for Daddy. He watched his herd closely, and was careful to be present whenever a cow was in distress having her calf. He developed equipment to help pull a calf when a cow couldn't deliver it herself. Whenever he had a cow that had calving problems, he kept a record of that cow and sold her and her calf in the fall. Once a cow had such problems, she was likely to have problems again, and her calf might have similar problems when grown.

The black cows all looked alike, so they wore silver ear tags that had numbers on them so we could tell them apart. I was particularly fond of cow Number 55. Lady

Ebonette was a registered Angus, and whenever I helped Daddy feed the cows she wandered up to the fence and waited until I scratched her forehead.

As Daddy heaved huge pitchforks of hay into the manger he recited, "I never saw a purple cow, I never hope to see one, but I can tell you anyhow, I'd rather see than be one."

But we did have a purple cow. The Purple People Eater was a cow so black it shimmered with a purple tint. She came by her name honestly, too. The Purple People Eater was just like the other cows in the barnyard most of the time. However, when she had a new calf, she was a good mom, a protective mom, and a dangerous mom. She charged anything that came close to her new calf. Daddy had to keep her in a corral until her calf grew enough to fend for itself.

Cows and Cats

Paul and David began to build a snow fort. The melting snow made perfect snowballs. Johnny and I worked on building the biggest snowman in history. The snow was too cold and powdery throughout the winter to make snowmen or have snowball fights, but now the snow was perfect for playing in.

Carolyn helped Johnny roll the base of the snowman. I rummaged through the vegetable bin for the perfect snowman carrot nose. I found a scarf and hat and ran to the coal shed to find the perfect pieces of coal for the eyes.

Before we could finish, it was time for chores, then supper.

"We'll finish tomorrow," Carolyn promised. "It's Saturday, so there's no school."

"Let's have a war!" David suggested. "We can build another fort, and bomb each other with snowballs!"

"I get to be on Paul's side!" I shouted. "Johnny is, too! Carolyn and David are the Germans!"

Just before bedtime, Daddy pulled the ashes from the coal stove and I helped him carry them behind the house to the ash pile. The air felt warm and still, and I looked at the crisp, starry sky.

"Look at the dancing lights!" I exclaimed.

Daddy looked at the northern sky. "They are the northern lights," he explained.

Long icicles were forming on the eves on the house as the night air dipped below the freezing point.

As I snuggled under my blankets and hugged my pink gingham bunny, I could hardly fall asleep, anticipating the fun we would have in the snow tomorrow.

Spring snow

I woke up early Saturday morning. I hugged my warm fuzzy blanket. Something was wrong. Johnny and Paul jumped out of bed, eager to start the snowball war. A chill penetrated the room. The fire in the oil stove roared, and the metal surface of the coal cook stove glowed red-hot in the kitchen, as Daddy had it stoked with hard coal. I climbed out of my crib. Icy snow sprayed against the windows as they rattled in the high winds from an unexpected blizzard.

Tears stung my eyes. Just when winter seemed to be leaving, it returned with a blast that left me numb. Even with the stoves burning hot, the floors were cold and the curtains rustled as the howling winds found their ways through the old panes.

Mom was in the kitchen kneading biscuit dough for breakfast. The windows had beautiful patterns painted by Jack Frost, but they did not impress me. I pressed my thumbnail and thumb knuckle against the window again and again, so it looked like Jack Frost had walked across his picture. I didn't like Jack Frost anymore. The temperatures had plummeted, and all that perfect snowball snow was now icy sheets. Fresh snow was falling and blowing, making visibility nearly nonexistent. We couldn't even finish our snowman!

The door flung open and a swirling fury of icy snow settled around Daddy as he closed the storm outside. My eyes grew round as saucers. Daddy cradled a wet newborn calf.

Calf needing help

"This little guy needs some help," he said.

He walked across the kitchen floor, leaving a snowy trail that quickly melted. Mom laid a soft old blanket on the floor next to the stove and Daddy carefully laid the shivering calf on it.

"Get some towels," he ordered.

Daddy let me help him wipe off the shivering baby calf with a thick towel, and he rubbed its legs and neck vigorously until it warmed up and stopped shaking. Mom heated a pan of warm milk and poured it into a pop-bottle. She stretched a black nipple Daddy had purchased at the drug store in the veterinary supply section, over the mouth of the bottle so the calf could get some warm nourishment.

"Can we keep it? He can stay in the boys' room! Please, Daddy?" I begged.

"No, he needs his mommy," Daddy said. "As soon as he's dry and his body temperature is normal, I'm going to take him back to his mother."

When the calf had warmed up, Daddy carried him to his mother in the barn and kept them both there until the storm was over and the weather warmed up outside.

"I hate winter," I complained to Daddy. "It wrecked all our plans!"

"Well," Daddy consoled me, "there's one thing that's good about a spring storm. The snow from a spring storm goes away soon. If we had this blizzard in October or November, we'd have six more months of winter to look forward to."

He had a point! I decided it wasn't as bad as I first thought, but I still wasn't happy.

Finally, the weather did become warmer. During the afternoons the melting snow flooded our gravel lane in the low places and made the Four Buttes Road almost too muddy to drive on.

As the snow gradually melted away, patches of earth were exposed on the hills and fuzzy crocuses finally showed their beautiful blooms in the pasture behind our house. Johnny and I wandered down to the grove of trees and ran and played in the brown, grassy hills. We picked bouquets of spring flowers for Mom to adorn the supper table.

Throughout the winter Mom had taken the laundry into town. As Mom worked at the newspaper office, the modern Laundromat with its automatic machines had the clothes spin-dried and ready to be brought home when she finished her business. She brought the wet clothes home and dried them in our electric tumble dryer.

Now that it was spring, she could do the laundry at home. One warm morning she wheeled the old wringer washing machine out of its corner. She put two rinse tubs on a bench next to it. We gathered all the clothes and sorted them according to color. She used the same water for the entire wash, so she started with the bed sheets, white underwear and shirts. Next, she washed the prints, the colors, and ended with the jeans and work clothes.

As the washing machine sloshed and mixed the clothes together in the sudsy water, I waited for the timer to ding.

Then Mom opened the cover and retrieved each article of clothing from the tub with a wooden stick, and fed it through the wringer.

I stood on a chair and directed the damp clothes to the first rinse tub. She loaded the washing tub again with the next batch of clothes. As the machine sloshed the load, we put the clothes in the rinse water through the wringer again. As the clothes fell into the second rinse tub, Mom watched to make sure the stubborn stains were gone from the newly-washed clothes. She guided the clothes through the wringer carefully once again, making sure the buttons were flat so they wouldn't pop off as they passed through the rolling cylinders. The clothes fell into the basket.

Once the load was through the second rinse tub, she carried the basket of damp clothes to the clothesline beside the house. I helped by handing her the clothes pins. The dry prairie wind whipped the sheets and fresh clothes, and by the time she finished hanging the load, the clothes she hung first were already dry. She watched the shirts and dresses, and gathered them while they were yet damp. She placed the damp clothes in a plastic bag and stored them in the refrigerator so they wouldn't mildew before she ironed them.

Once the line-dried sheets, towels and underwear were folded and put away, Mom got the ironing board from the corner. She placed the plastic bag of damp clothes from the refrigerator on the floor and ironed the damp clothes so they were crisp and perfect.

Chapter 8
End of School

I loved playing outdoors in the springtime. The weather wasn't too cold like it was in the winter, and it wasn't too hot like it was in the summer. Spring was a joyful time, bursting with life and promise after the long cold winter.

The fuzzy purple spring crocuses covered the hills and the grass turned green. The cattle roamed around the barnyard, and the baby calves scampered about, playing their games of chase.

One Saturday morning Daddy announced, "The cows have all had their calves and this would be a good day to put them down in the big pasture. Who's going to help?"

There was no lack of volunteers for this job. We thought chasing cows was fun. Every spring we drove the cows and baby calves to the summer pasture, which had spring-fed ponds and plenty of grass. Once there, they required little attention except an occasional count to make sure none had gone through a fence and strayed away.

We all participated in the cattle drive. From the barnyard it was about two miles to the big pasture, but we had to go through some open fields and cross the county road.

Carolyn's horse, Patch, seemed to know when there was work to be done. Carolyn found Patch hiding behind the barn. With the bridle hidden behind her back, she lured him close with a juicy carrot in her open hand. She moved slowly, being careful not to startle him. When his nose reached for the carrot, she slipped the reins around his neck. She placed another carrot piece in her hand, along with the bridle bit. When Patch's lips reached for the second carrot, she quickly slipped the bit in his mouth and pulled the bridle over his head as he munched noisily on the crisp treat. She always caught her horse this way, and no matter how much Patch didn't want to be ridden, he fell for the same trick every time.

Carolyn flapped the saddle blanket on top of Patch's back and hoisted the old deep-seated western saddle over his withers. She pulled the cinch tight to hold the saddle on Patch's round back, and mounted him. Riding Patch, Carolyn could bring back any cow that decided to head in the wrong direction.

The rest of us walked beside and behind the cows, keeping them moving toward the pasture. David carried a six-foot bull whip that he cracked expertly in mid-air. It was the same sound I heard on the radio when the show, "Rawhide," was on.

Paul carried a lariat, twirling it overhead, ready to rope any strays. Daddy drove the pickup truck, and went ahead to swing the barbed wire gates wide open so the cattle wouldn't get tangled in them. I pretended we were on a long cattle drive to Texas. In a few weeks we would have to bring the cows back to the corrals to brand the calves, but Daddy liked them to get a little bigger before branding their little behinds with the great big branding irons.

Daddy had ordered one hundred baby chicks, and now the downy yellow chicks were chirping under the heat lamps in the chicken coop. A couple new piglets were squealing in the pigpen next to the old outhouse.

Our kitty population was dwindling, and a family that lived in town offered us a mother cat and a litter of kittens they wanted to get rid of. We brought the batch of kitties home and found a warm place in the hay shed beside the milking stalls for them. I spent hours in the shed playing with the adorable kittens.

We brought a black-and-copper tortoiseshell kitten into the house to help keep the mouse population down. Inky never did choose to be my baby, so she found a home with the barn cats. Grandpa named the tortoiseshell kitten "Rusty," and she became the chief cat forever.

Dixie was nowhere to be found. Tina was gone, too. I called and called the dogs, but there was no response. As I went by the feed granary on the way to the outhouse, I heard a whimpering cry.

"That's it!" I thought. "Dixie must be under the granary."

The granary sat on stones and earth. I crawled underneath, pulling myself with my elbows. When I got to the very end of the crawlspace, my eyes adjusted to the dark hole. There was Dixie with ten squirming puppies. They were tiny, with eyes squinted shut. Dixie, smiling from ear to ear, lay as her puppies nursed. A couple days later Tina showed up. She was behind the barn with her new litter of puppies. There were seventeen puppies in all.

Puppies and Cousins

Tina saw Dixie's beautiful litter, and when Dixie was taking a "cat-nap," she dog-napped one. Carrying the sleepy puppy by the neck, she introduced it to her litter. When Dixie realized Tina had stolen her puppy, she went to rescue it, bringing back one of Tina's puppies, instead. By the time the puppies were running around, nobody was sure which puppies belonged to which dog.

The unthinkable finally happened. The dogs grew in size, and word got out to the neighborhood that we had puppies. We populated most of the countryside with these fine-tempered dogs. I wanted to keep them all. I resented each intruder that drove away with one of my puppies.

There were only three puppies left. Johnny and I were making mountains in the "hole" when I saw an unfamiliar car slowly drive up our lane. I was used to seeing unfamiliar cars. Over the past two weeks, fourteen unfamiliar cars with strangers drove away with my puppies. I ran to the house. Mom was finishing the breakfast dishes.

"Mom!" I yelled. "Someone's coming!"

She grabbed a towel to dry her hands and told me to find the puppies quickly. Reluctantly, I went outside.

A pretty lady parked her car behind our white station wagon. A baby and a little boy were with her. I loved babies, but not this one. I scowled at the lady and the boy as they got out of the car.

Two of the puppies scampered up to greet them. I didn't even attempt to find the third. What if she took all three?

Mom had to remind me of my manners when I informed the would-be dog owner that the rest of the dogs were all mine, so they should go now.

The little boy picked up the black and white puppy.

"This one, Mommy!" he exclaimed.

His mother smiled approvingly.

Mom invited them into the house, and offered them coffee, milk and cake. The little boy held his new found friend like his mother was holding the baby. He carried the puppy into the house. Mom didn't allow dogs in the house, but she didn't say anything.

As they stood up to leave, the woman didn't realize her baby had spit up on the kitchen floor! Mom walked them out to the car and thanked them for giving the puppy a home.

When she came in, I exclaimed, "Mom, look what the baby did! And that lady didn't even offer to wipe it up!"

Mom took a towel and, as she wiped up the mess, she simply stated, "Babies do that sometimes."

I wouldn't know. I never had a baby around. I was the youngest. But now, I decided, if babies make this kind of mess, maybe having a baby would be more trouble than it was worth!

It was near the end of May. Daddy was finishing his rounds in the fields seeding his oats, barley, and spring wheat. Grandpa was getting the garden ready to plant. Mom planted the peas, beans, radishes, carrots, rutabagas and lettuce.

Grandpa had the corn planter and the potato planter ready. Daddy made two passes with his tractor-pulled tool bar, and Paul and David helped Grandpa measure the width of the rows so he could plant a tidy garden.

The corn patch and potato patch alternated locations each year. This year the potato patch was going to be close, next to the garden with the peas and beans. Grandpa planned to plant the corn at the far end of the garden, near the "big shed."

Grandpa sat on a bucket as he cut the purple-treated seed potatoes with his jackknife. Each chunk had to have at least two "eyes," because the "eyes" sprouted to make the new plant. Careful to get a couple "eyes" in each chunk, he quartered the small purple-tinted potatoes. When he had a bucket full, he poured them into a pouch made from an old gunnysack that he wore so he could carry the "seeds" with him. He took the potato planter and began planting in the row where the beans ended. When he planted the potato patch, he brought out the corn planter.

The corn planter was made from two boards with a hinged clam-shaped shovel at the bottom, and handles on the top. An attached metal can dispensed corn into the nose of the planter, just a few kernels at a time. The clam-like shovel opened when Grandpa pressed the boards together at the top, depositing the seed corn into the soft earth. While holding the handles at the top of the planter, Grandpa stepped on the foot piece on the bottom, pushing the clam-nose of the planter into the soil. As he slapped the boards together at the top, the clam-shaped nose opened, depositing the seed corn. He then pulled the planter out of the ground and stepped the planter into the next spot, depositing seed into the earth six inches from the last. The corn planter looked like a leg brace as it moved with Grandpa's leg down the row in a rhythmic pattern: shove into the ground, slap the boards together, pull the planter out, open, shove, slap, out, open, shove, slap, out, until he reached the end of the row. He came back again without missing a beat.

Sometimes he let Johnny and me walk with him, and we carried a bag of corn seed so he would never run out. He told us we were a big help as we talked and worked beside him.

Springtime kept us busy. The distant popping of the old model G John Deere tractor and the pungent smell of manure told us that Daddy and Grandpa were cleaning the barn and cattle shed of the winter's dung accumulation. Daddy drove the old tractor with its attached farmhand, and lifted huge loads of the manure into the waiting dump truck box.

As Daddy moved the levers on the control, the hydraulic arms reached high above the truck. The heavy load rocked the truck as it landed in the truck box.

David was pulling the plow behind the Minneapolis-Moline tractor in a nearby summer fallow field, mixing piles of manure into the sandy soil. No odor-free chemical fertilizer could compare with this natural kind.

Mom hid herself in the house with the windows shut to keep the odor from penetrating the furniture fabric, curtains, and bedding. There would be no laundry hanging out to dry today.

The last day of school was finally here. The teacher, students, and all our mothers drove to the nearby Buttes for a picnic. The Buttes are four rocky hills that can be seen for miles and are a well-known landmark. Many years earlier they were known as the "Whiskey Buttes," because the early-day fur traders used to meet Indian trappers there to exchange illicit whiskey for furs. The little town of Four Buttes was named after the landmark.

Ladies at School Picnic

Our mothers brought picnic baskets packed with our lunches. We piled into the cars and drove to the first butte. We helped set out the blankets and baskets, and then ran off, excited about running in the hills and having fun with our friends one last time before summer vacation.

We enjoyed sandwiches, cold fried chicken, Kool-Aid and cookies. We played games and explored the little crevices and caves that we imagined were the dens of "bad guys" in " the olden days." Of course, we moved suspicious rocks, hoping to unearth some hidden treasures.

In a community of farmers, the church took a break from Sunday School classes once school was dismissed. It was marked with a wonderful Sunday School picnic filled with a long table of potluck dishes. Races and games were planned for the entire afternoon. Horseshoes were tossed, three legged races, relays, high jump, long jump, and egg toss games were played. Chet Murphy lived near the river, and graciously hosted our large church family for this spring event. The big boys explored the bank of the river, and sometimes brought back a treasure such as a water snake or some other creature.

Sunday School Picnic

Chapter 9

Glasgow Air Force Base

The warm, breezy days of summer again settled on the prairie. The big sky stretched from horizon to horizon like a huge dome. There wasn't a cloud in sight.

Paul joined Johnny and me in the hole. None of my friends had a sandbox like the hole. Because it was an old well filled in with sand, there was no bottom to limit our digging. We dug deep in the earth to make foxholes that we could hide in like Daddy did during the war with his folding army spade.

A meadowlark chirped his beautiful tune nearby. A crow cawed, and a lone killdeer perched on the telephone wire overhead cried its name with its high-pitched voice, "Killdeeeer, killdeeeer."

Carolyn walked out of the yard and down the lane. She was a "rock hound", and loved going on long walks to find see-through Montana agates. Cookie, one of Dixie's playful puppies, was working his way into Carolyn's heart as he circled her legs and trotted beside her.

I busied myself with my brothers, helping to dig the foxholes in our "combat area." Suddenly a frightened Dixie jumped in a newly-dug foxhole and an ear-shattering "BOOM, BOOM" made us believe our tranquil make-believe "war zone" had indeed become part of World War II.

The thunderous announcement unexpectedly interrupted our war as two jet planes from the nearby Glasgow Air Base broke the sound barrier and scribbled their white vapor trails across the summer sky. I ran to the house, screaming in terror, and Mom tried to comfort me.

"It's just the air force pilots practicing, just in case we go to war again," she explained.

I didn't like it. She encouraged me to go back outside. I was reluctant, but as I watched the tiny silver jets drawing the white, puffy trail across the sky, it looked as though they wouldn't be back soon. Dixie climbed out of the foxhole, and I figured it must be safe. She was even more of a coward than I when it came to thunderstorms, fireworks, or sonic booms.

The jets made passes across the sky frequently those days, and each sonic boom caused me to cry in terror and run to Mom's apron. Finally, Daddy and Mom decided there would be only one way for me to conquer my fear. I'd have to face it.

One Saturday morning Daddy woke us up early.

"Who wants to go to the Glasgow Air Force Base?" he asked.

Going anywhere sounded like fun to us, so five excited children dressed quickly as Mom prepared a picnic lunch. Paul told me this was going to be a long drive, longer even than going to Wolf Point or Plentywood. We didn't go on long trips often, and a two-hour drive in the car was longer than any other trip I'd ever been on.

We drove past all the familiar neighboring farms and finally crested the hill just past Peerless. We were on the horizon where the sun set each evening. I had never been past the horizon. Behind us, Daddy pointed to the horizon where our farm was, ten miles away. The house and trees looked like miniature toys. In front of us spread miles and miles of fresh prairie, with pastures bordering massive fields. Strips of brown summer fallow alternated with green strips of newly-sprouted wheat.

The road past Peerless wasn't paved then, and the dust behind us stayed suspended in the still morning air like the vapor trail of the jets as they crossed the sky. After we turned south past Opheim, another small town forty miles from home, we found ourselves on a paved road again. We drove for what seemed to be hours to me. Each hill brought a new scene, but each scene was similar to the last, and I was getting bored. Finally, in the distance, we saw red and white candy-striped balls on red-and-white candy-striped sticks.

"What are those?" I asked.

"Those are water towers for the base," Daddy answered.

"Then we're almost there," I reasoned.

"We're getting closer, but we are still several miles away," Daddy said.

As we approached the base our excitement grew, but so did the traffic. We pulled up behind a line of cars and waited our turn to get in the gate. The line coming from Glasgow, a town south of the base and much larger than Scobey, was twice as long. I'd never seen so many cars, even at the county fair. I knew this must be an important event for so many people to come to it.

Once a year the Glasgow Air Force Base had an open house. They treated the public to a display of Air Force jets, bombers, tanks, and other equipment. Air shows were scheduled throughout the day. Pilots stood by their aircraft to answer people's questions.

Mom stood on the wide cement runway, looking at the massive jets. I buried my face in her skirt, realizing the jets that flew overhead were indeed frightful machines. She pointed at the silver, streamlined fighter jet and asked if I'd like to see what it looked like inside. Johnny sure did, so I followed.

Inside the plane were benches and harness straps to secure the airmen. It looked cold and uncomfortable. There were no decorations or anything else to make it look pretty. I decided it must be that way because the flyers were just men, and moms are the people that make things look pretty.

The pilot and copilot's seats were more comfortable-looking than the others, and the pilot let Johnny sit in the seat and touch the levers. There were bunches of gas gauges, clocks, and dials on the dash board. I wanted to know what they were all for, but a long line was forming outside the aircraft and it was time for us to move on.

Inside one of the hangers was a B-52. We had heard more about the B-52 than any other aircraft, and Johnny was awestruck. His eyes grew round as saucers and his mouth formed a silent, "Wow."

A jolly man came up to us and knelt down in front of Johnny. "Do you like it, son?" he asked my obviously-impressed big brother. "How would you like to put on the vest and parachute I wear when I fly it?"

Johnny couldn't talk. He just nodded, and the man laughed. He draped the vest over my brother's shoulders, and put the large, man-sized helmet on his little boy head, and took a Polaroid picture of him.

Johnny B-52 gear

"There you go, son," he said as he handed Johnny the blank picture. Mom and I watched as Johnny's form appeared on the picture. Soon the details were clear. The man took the picture back and wiped it with a smelly solution so the picture would stop developing. When the picture was dry, he gave it back to Johnny.

"Always remember me when you look at that picture," he told him.

Johnny finally managed to say, "Thank you," and walked away with the greatest treasure anyone had ever given him.

"I want one too," I cried as we left, but Mom, in her wisdom, realized this was Johnny's special moment. She assured me that I could be first in line to see the giant cargo plane.

As the sun began to sink behind the distant horizon we gathered at the car. We'd had a full day, and I was tired. As Daddy drove down the highway, the rhythm of the car going over bumps in the road, the soft music that came over the scratchy radio, and the chattering of David and Paul soon faded. I closed my eyes.

A sudden loud "BOOM" woke me up. It was morning, and I was safe in my crib. I heard the faint roar of a jet, but I wasn't scared anymore. I would never again be afraid of those tiny silver jets with the white vapor trails and the big "booms" that had once shattered my security.

The jets were big, but the men that drove them were nice, just like Daddy, and now I knew those jets high in the sky would never hurt me.

Glasgow air show

Chapter 10

Peerless Boys

School was already a distant memory. It had been more than two weeks since the last day of school, and we were free. Even with gardening, field work, and the various chores expected of us, we no longer had the strict schedule of school all day. However, now it was time for Vacation Bible School.

We lived half way between Scobey, which was the county seat, and a very small town named Peerless. From our house we could see Peerless, ten miles away on the horizon. In between, in a lower area known as "the flat," were small groves of trees that marked the locations of the farms where our neighbors lived. Because of Daddy's involvement in school boards, farm and civic organizations and the Lutheran Church, he knew everybody.

An invisible line across the flats divided the school districts and communities of Four Buttes and Peerless. If you lived on our side of the line, you attended school in Four Buttes or Scobey, were in the Scobey telephone exchange, and attended church in Scobey. If you were on the other side, you attended school in Peerless, had to telephone long distance to Four Buttes and Scobey, and probably went to church in Peerless.

Although small, Peerless had a high school and a Catholic and Lutheran church. Most of the children on the flat were in the Scobey school district, but some attended school and church in Peerless.

The Scobey pastor and intern pastor served the Peerless Lutheran Church, too, and we had our choice of attending Vacation Bible School in either Scobey or Peerless. This year the Shipsteads decided to go to Vacation Bible School in Peerless, and we did too. I wanted to be with Kristi.

They held the Bible school in the Peerless High School building. Most of the children there were strangers to me. I knew only two of the Peerless families. One was the Andersen family, who we occasionally visited. The Andersen's had five children, just like our family, and they were close to us in age. Jewel Andersen was my friend.

Vacation Bible School offered many fun activities, crafts, and games. We learned about Jesus and sang hymns that the grownups sang in church, but we didn't sing the ones that droned. We sang the fun songs like "What a Friend We Have in Jesus," "Fairest Lord Jesus," and "I Love to Tell the Story." I wasn't sure what story we were to tell, so the teacher explained it was the story of Jesus and how he came to earth to die for our sins. My favorite song was "Onward Christian Soldiers," because I liked the idea of being a soldier like Daddy.

During craft time the older children made bookends of wood tiles and plaster. They shaped them like the stained-glass windows in the big church in Scobey. The crafts we younger children made weren't nearly as fancy, but they were more colorful. We made stained glass windows out of colored plastic framed with construction paper.

During recess and lunch hour we played outside. The Peerless school had a merry-go-round and plenty of swings. We played tag until one day when the big boys decided it was more fun to just chase the girls. Wallace and Jimmy chased Kristi, Jewel and me. They didn't want to catch us; the fun was in the chase. I thought it was fun the first recess, but the next recess Wallace frightened me.

"I'm going to eat you up!" he declared with a menacing growl as he came after us. Kristi and Jewel laughed, running as fast as they could. They knew the boys were just teasing. I was terrified, and every recess became more terrifying. Finally, Wallace came out brandishing a plastic fork. He was enjoying this game because I believed him.

Johnny didn't care about chasing the girls, so he played on the swings with some other boys. I decided Peerless wasn't the best place to go to Bible school after all. As much as I had looked forward to Vacation Bible School, I was glad when it was over.

I discussed it with Johnny as we worked in our "garden plot," planting imaginary potatoes and corn in "the hole."

"Wallace and Jimmy were bad," I declared. "They said they were going to eat me, and they chased me every recess."

"They are really nice boys and were just having fun teasing you," Johnny explained.

As we played in the sand a sudden gust of blowing dirt and tumble weeds came swirling through the yard, filling my eyes with sand and frightening me. I ran screaming to the house, and as Mom worked to get the sand out of my eyes, she told me that was just a "dust devil." When the cool prairie air meets a pocket of hot air, the two air masses swirl, forming these whirlwinds. They are strong winds, but usually no more than a nuisance to children playing in the yard

Playing in the hole

Chapter 11

The New Room

Our house was too small. The small living room served as my parents' bedroom and the nursery. I was the baby, still in a crib. There was nowhere else to put me.

Heavy machinery was coming today. Daddy was planning a big surprise. Johnny and I went to Kristi's house to spend the night so we would be out of the way. Grandpa, Paul, and David would help Daddy, but we were too little.

Penny, Kathy, and Kristi

I loved staying at Kristi's house. She lived in a new, modern ranch house with hardwood floors that we slid across in our stocking feet. Her house was uncluttered, and the beds were made with new matching bedspreads. The sturdy dressers matched the beds. Each person had his or her own dresser. The sliding doors on the closets rolled easily on their tracks, and there was enough room in the closets for everybody's dresses and shirts to hang freely and uncrowded.

Jimmy, Kristi's brother, was tending a fire near the shop. Johnny and I were intrigued with the fire. We were never allowed to play around fire like that. Jimmy had a tin can of liquid that looked like water. Whenever he sprinkled the "water" in the fire, it exploded into big high flames, and then died down again.

"Wow! I thought water always put fire out!" I exclaimed.

"This is magic water," Jimmy teased.

"What is it?" Johnny asked.

"It's gas," Kristi exclaimed, "and you're not allowed to do that! I'm telling!"

"No!" Jimmy appealed. "Daddy knows I'm doing this," he fibbed. "Anyway, the gas is almost gone." And he threw the last bit of fuel on the fire and the flames once again leaped high toward the sky. The fire died down and Jimmy covered it with dirt to assure that it wouldn't reignite.

"Let's go swing." Kristi and I ran and claimed our swings. Johnny and Jimmy went to the large steel Quonset building where their dad, Big Jim kept his equipment. Big Jim was in the Quonset working on his new tractor.

At noon, Barbee called us in for lunch. My mom cooked with few spices, and she even cooked part of the chili without chili seasoning or onions because that was the only way Johnny would eat it. She also baked casseroles with nothing extra added, and everything was a bit bland, just like we liked it. Barbee was skilled at using peppery spices. The steam curled from the fragrant vegetable soup as we sat in our places next to our friends.

Barbee was bouncy and had an obvious appreciation for small children. I looked at the meal, and gingerly took an open-faced tuna sandwich, hoping no one would notice I wasn't filling my bowl with that spicy soup.

Penny noticed. "Have some soup, Kathy!" she offered.

"I don't want any."

"Go ahead. It's good!"

"I don't like it."

Penny was obviously shocked by my blunt honesty. Barbee put a little in my bowl, and I sipped it reluctantly, along with a soft piece of buttered bread.

Towards the end of the meal, Big Jim leaned back on his chair and lighted his cherry tobacco pipe and puffed a ring of fragrant smoke.

"What's your middle name, Kathy?" Barbee inquired.

"Um, I'm not sure, but I think it's Run." Everyone laughed. I blushed, and began to shrink under the table.

"Kathy Run. Well, I'll be," she exclaimed. And from that day on, even though Mom told me my name was Kathryn Lynn Rustebakke, Barbee and all her girls called me Kathy Run.

Finally dinner was over. Kristi and I went to the living room to watch "Flipper" on their black and white television set.

Penny cornered me. "Didn't your parents ever teach you manners?"

Just recently Daddy had been concerned about our table manners, so he decided once a week we would eat at the formal oak table and practice eating properly with formal dinnerware.

"Yep, we practice manners at the big table in the living room," I informed her proudly, unsure of her motive for questioning me.

"Well, it's not good manners to tell people you don't like dinner," she said.

"Oh. What do you do if you don't like it?"

"Well, you take a little, and tell them how good it is. Then say something like, 'I'm full' or something."

When Onalee and Penny completed the dishes it was time for afternoon naps. Barbee was going to have a card party this evening, so Penny and Onalee were going to help set up the card tables and prepare snacks and decorate for the party. Mom gave up on giving me naps before I was two years old. I couldn't imagine having to sleep when it was broad daylight outside. I submitted to Shipstead's customs, and waited, hoping this quiet time would soon be over. Kristi quickly fell sound asleep. Soon I had enough and wandered into the living room.

"I can't sleep," I told Barbee.

"Go back to bed, and try," she answered.

Five minutes later I got up again. "I still can't sleep, Barbee."

"Go back to bed," she ordered.

Three minutes passed. It seemed like three hours. I got up again.

"If you go to sleep," Penny promised, "I'll make you a popcorn surprise." She was folding paper, making little "nut cups" for the party.

I went back to bed. Minutes later my eyes popped open. Kristi was still sleeping. I fell asleep too! I jumped out of bed.

"I slept!" I exclaimed.

"No you didn't!" Penny argued.

"Yes, I did! I closed my eyes and slept really fast!"

Barbee realized I wasn't going to fall asleep. Whether she believed that I fell asleep or not, she saw how seriously I believed I slept. She told Penny to give me my surprise.

Penny rolled her eyes and half-filled the "nut cup" with a small amount of popcorn and raisins. She wasn't happy giving in to me. Her mom was strict, and she would have never gotten away with a two-minute nap.

Kristi and I helped set up for the party. We watched as Penny decorated a sign. She carefully printed:

"WELCOME!"

"WELL, COME!"

We handed tape to Penny as she taped the welcome sign to the front door.

How we wished we could stay up and be a part of the party. Tonight, was the first time Penny was allowed to stay up. The party started at eight, and we had to be in be bed sleeping before the guests arrived.

After supper we prepared for bath time. Kristi had an indoor bathroom with double sinks and a big slippery bathtub. We soaped up, and Barbee washed our hair, more carefully than my mom to keep the soap from our eyes. When the first guests arrived, we were tucked into bed, and as Onalee read "Cinderella," I closed my eyes and fell fast asleep before the stepsisters left for the ball.

Daddy and Mom came to get us the next day. We had had a good time at the Shipstead's house, but I was anxious to go home before nap time again.

As we drove up our lane, I saw what the men were doing. Another house, or part of it, was sitting next to our house on big tires. Kristi's parents had built a new house that replaced an old farm house. A section of her old house had been pulled by a big tractor all the way to our place, and the partial building sat in our yard.

Daddy was digging a basement, and as soon as it was finished and concrete was poured for the walls and floor, this new house would be attached to ours, giving us a larger living room and a new sun porch.

As the weeks passed, the work was completed, and Mom chose a new carpet to complete the room. Mom said we would get the sun porch ready for me next year and I could have my very own room.

New room

Preparing to attach new room

Chapter 12
Relatives

Kristi and I were "shirt-tail" cousins. At least that's what everyone called us. Her dad's brother, Uncle Bud, married my dad's sister, Auntie Annette. My cousins, Gary, Mark, and Jeffrey were her cousins, too. We weren't sure how this worked, but we were related, and so I claimed all Kristi's cousins, aunts and uncles and her grandma as my own as well. Mom's parents had both passed away, and she only had an older adopted brother who never came to visit from his home in Washington State because his wife didn't like to travel.

Mom was a welcomed surprise to her parents when she came along, as they had long ago given up hope of having children of their own. Mom had several cousins, but they, as well as her brother's family, lived in other states and I never got to know any of them except Mom's Aunt Daisy and her daughter, Marguerite.

Aunt Daisy was a stout woman, a retired schoolmarm, and she expected us to behave when she was around. She took it upon herself to get us to "toe-the-line," since she thought Mom was too lenient. We tried to be polite, but we were always relieved when she decided to go home. Cousin Marguerite was Mom's age and very talkative. Mom loved their visits, but I did not.

Mom's dad, who was born in Pennsylvania, had been raised in Pennsylvania and New York. He was still in his teens when both of his parents died in the typhoid fever epidemic. As the oldest, he had to work to support his five younger brothers and sisters. Later he moved to Washington State to work in the lumber mills.

Mom was born and raised in Tacoma, where there were tall buildings, public transportation, electricity, and neighborhood gangs. The gangs, though, weren't like the big city gangs like in "West Side Story." They were simply groups of neighborhood kids that played together and enjoyed such games as hopscotch, jacks, baseball, roller-skate hockey, and cowboys and Indians.

During World War II, Tacoma was actively involved in the war effort. Mom attended college then and also worked part time. During summer vacations she worked at the Seattle-Tacoma shipyards. She told us stories about how the city was blacked out at night to hide from possible attacks by enemy aircraft.

At a USO (United Service Organization) dance for servicemen she met the tall, handsome, Montana man she later married. After the war, that handsome soldier came back for her. After the beautiful wedding, she abandoned her modern lifestyle to live on a remote Montana homestead with no running water, electricity, indoor bathroom, or telephone service.

Many of the young soldiers that returned from the war were married the same year my parents were married, and they started their families soon after.

Daddy was born in northeastern Montana where we lived, but spent most of his first ten years living near Thief River Falls, Minnesota. Several of his relatives still lived there.

Daddy had an older brother, Homer, and a younger sister. Annette was married to Uncle Bud. Uncle Bud was also Kristi's uncle, and he and Annette lived on a ranch about ten miles away. They had three boys. Gary was Carolyn's age. Mark was a little younger than Paul, and Jeffrey was almost my age, but I was still older than him --twenty days older.

In 1941, Daddy was debating whether he should volunteer for the army. He volunteered for the draft, and was the first to be drafted from our county under the Selective Service, and was stationed at Fort, Lewis, Washington when Pearl Harbor was attacked. He met Mom while stationed at Fort Lewis, and their romance began to grow. In January 1943, my mother tearfully said goodbye as he was sent to Fort Gordon Johnson in Florida and to Camp Picke in Virginia for additional training. He then was sent to overseas.

He joined the Second Ranger Battalion while stationed in England, and participated in the famous D-day Invasion at Normandy Beach on June 6, 1944. He was shot in his abdomen as he waded to shore from the landing craft and spent the next six months in army hospitals in England. He returned to his outfit during the Battle of the Bulge. When the war was over, he went through the horrible concentration camps to make sure everything was cleared out. Finally, his papers came through, and he was able to come home, married my mother, and bought a farm next to Grandpa's farm.

For the latter half of his childhood Daddy and his family had lived in a little house a mile east of the house where I grew up. Daddy's uncle had homesteaded the place. We children loved rummaging through the buildings at "Grandpa's old place." The house still had the old kitchen stove and some of the furniture and dishes that Grandma had used. Daddy and Uncle Homer had stayed in the bunk house, a shack separate from the farm house. We found letters and books from the past, and always imagined our handsome bachelor uncle to be quite popular with the young ladies, so hoped to find old love letters he may have left behind.

The cook car that was used to feed the crews during harvest time still was equipped with a stove, table, and shelves. Harnesses, tools, and various artifacts cluttered the wagon. The paddles of the tall windmill still turned-on windy days, but the pipes weren't connected, so water no longer filled the big round wooden water tank as it once did.

Grandpa now lived in Scobey in a little yellow house with green shutters. Grandma had passed away when I was almost five years old. I remembered her Sunday visits and the orange, yellow, and white candy corn that I called "grandma candy." I remembered her at church, and how she loved visiting with friends, like her next-door neighbor, Eleanor Hagen. She loved flowers, especially the yellow rose bushes and hollyhocks around her house and the blooms in her backyard flower garden. They were still there, a memorial of her life. She also loved to knit, and the royal blue scarf she had knitted for me was my special treasure. As I grew, my memory of her began to fade, so I held the things that reminded me of her close to my heart.

Uncle Homer was my favorite person in the whole wide world, next to Mom and Daddy. He lived in Schenectady, New York, and worked for General Electric. He had ridden the box cars and hitchhiked to go to college during the difficult years of the great Depression. He was an educated man, and had one of those jobs that didn't make sense when he told us what he did, so we knew he must be important. And he was rich. When he visited, he always brought the most wonderful gifts.

Uncle Homer came for one of his visits and Johnny and I couldn't wait to see him. He had stayed in town with Grandpa the night before because he had driven all the way from New York, and he was tired.

Johnny and I could hardly wait to see him. Mom was busy cleaning the house and making pies, because Uncle

Homer loved pie. We waited until midmorning before driving to town. David said we had to get to him first, because Auntie Annette would want him at her house half the time.

When we got to Grandpa's house, we found Grandpa opening a can of peaches to go with the poached eggs and toast he was preparing for Uncle Homer's breakfast. Uncle Homer was a vegetarian, so we knew he wouldn't want bacon or sausage with his breakfast.

The fresh morning air flowed freely through the screen door.

"He's still sleeping," Grandpa said as we approached the door.

We tiptoed in, trying to be as quiet as five children who wanted to see their favorite Uncle could be.

Johnny sneaked into the living room, and peeked into Uncle Homer's room. He came back and said, "It's Uncle Homer, all right! Nobody else in the whole wide world has feet that big!"

I ran in to see, and giggled. "You're right, Johnny! He does have big feet."

Uncle Homer opened one eye. He wiggled his toe at me, and said, "This can't be Kathy, can it?" He propped up on his elbows. "If you'll give me ten minutes, I'll get ready, then we can really talk."

As he sat at the breakfast table, he sized us up. "Why, Johnny! You are really growing. Is your name Henry?"

"No," Johnny giggled. He knew he meant the poet, Henry Wadsworth Longfellow. Uncle Homer always said the boys were "Longfellows" when they grew taller.

"David, do you know why I'm so short?" he asked.

"You're not short." David responded. He knew Uncle Homer was taller than Daddy, and Daddy was over six feet tall.

"Well," he laughed, "just imagine how much taller I'd be if I didn't have so much turned over for feet!"

Our comments never embarrassed Uncle Homer. He had big feet, big ears, a big nose, and a big chin, but somehow, everything fit together and made the handsomest, kindest Uncle anyone could ever ask for.

He showed up with a surprise every time he came. This time he had a car for Daddy. Uncle Homer thought it would be easier on Mom if Daddy had his own car to drive around in so she could use the station wagon for things Moms need cars for. He had also brought coins for each child that were wrapped in plastic.

"Oh, goody!" I exclaimed! "Now I can get a Brown Cow!" I loved the chocolate, caramel lollipops. Brown Cows lasted forever, and they only cost a nickel!

"No, no," Uncle Homer said. "Here's some money if you want to buy candy."

He reached in his pocket and brought out a leather coin purse full of coins. My eyes grew round as saucers. I looked at Daddy and he nodded that I was allowed. I slowly picked out three coins so I wouldn't appear greedy.

Uncle Homer explained, "These plastic-covered coins are called proofs. They have never been touched by human hands, and if you hang onto them, they'll be worth some money someday."

It all seemed too serious for me. I could count money now, and these proofs may be worth a lot someday, but today the half-dollar, quarter, dime, nickel and penny that were in each of the proofs were worth ninety-one cents, and that seemed like enough to me.

When Homer finished breakfast, he started planning who he would visit. Soon, Auntie Annette and the boys arrived. Homer showed them the coins and I repeated Uncle Homer's explanation. "They've never been touched by human hands!"

Annette joked, "I knew monkeys were good for something! They must use monkey hands to wrap the coins!"

As the cousins looked over their proof sets, the grownups planned where Homer would go, what meals would be together with all of us, and when he could be free to visit some old friends that he hadn't seen for a long time.

Uncle Homer came to spend the first two days with us. We loved to play with Uncle Homer, and he never seemed to tire from our jokes and constant chatter.

Daddy saw when Uncle Homer needed a break; then he told us to play outside so the grownups could talk. Homer enjoyed going on walks and examining the rocks along the lane. We looked hard for agates, but I was sure

Carolyn already found all of them on our lane. Uncle Homer had an eye for beautiful things, and spotted several beautiful agates. Johnny and I scurried to pick them up for him, since he was so far from the ground.

Homer often carried his camera with him, and caught each of us doing things that were uniquely us. He loved the Montana sunsets, and each evening evaluated the sunset, as to whether it was worthy of being photographed.

After supper we gathered in the new living room, and Uncle Homer set up his slide projector. We enjoyed a slide show he put together from past visits. The slide show included Mom and Daddy's early years, when Daddy was still in the army. I thought Daddy was the most handsome soldier in the world, and Mom looked so eloquent with her beautiful long red hair braided and wrapped around her head like a crown. He had photos of Mom's parents in Tacoma, and photos of our house when it still looked like a homestead shanty. There were pictures from when Carolyn was a baby, all the way to pictures of me when I was a baby. And throughout the slide presentation Uncle Homer displayed the slides he had taken through the years of the colorful sunsets.

There were certain things Uncle Homer liked especially well. One was my mom's homemade chess pie. Another was freshly squeezed lemonade.

Mom needed some groceries, so Carolyn and Daddy prepared to drive to town. Lemons were expensive and Uncle Homer realized he just wouldn't get enough lemonade competing with all five of us kids for a taste. So, he gave Carolyn five whole dollars and said, "Buy as many lemons as you can. Spend it all!"

For five dollars, Carolyn brought home dozens of lemons. For the rest of Uncle Homer's stay Mom made sure the lemons were squeezed and fresh lemonade always sat in the refrigerator, ready for Uncle Homer.

After a couple days at our house, Homer went to stay with Auntie Annette and Uncle Bud. We were invited to a picnic at their house on the last evening.

Daddy was getting ready to cut the hayfield for the hay. Grandpa, who normally worked with Dad on the farm, went to spend the day with Uncle Homer. Daddy had to make sure the sickles were sharp enough to slice through the tall grass that would feed the cattle through the next winter.

Mom had to go to town to spend some time working at the newspaper office. We children all went to town with her to spend the afternoon at the park. The park was a favorite spot for Johnny and me. While the big kids swam in the big swimming pool, we splashed in the round kiddie pool. Johnny was old enough to go to the big swimming pool, but he didn't swim yet, and he felt safer in the little pool with me.

The pretty lifeguard waded in the shallow water, perfecting her golden tan as we splashed and squealed. The drain, the deepest part, was in the center of the round pool. It was just deep enough that we could do the dead man's float, but still reach the bottom with our arms. We pulled ourselves along, kicking our feet and pulling ourselves along with our hands. It almost looked like we were swimming.

When the pools closed Carolyn came over from the big pool to get us. We were to walk to Grandpa's house to wait for Mom.

"I swam the length!" David boasted. That meant he could swim in the deep end of the pool.

"I swam the length too!" I exclaimed.

"The little kid's pool doesn't have a length." David argued. "It's round!"

"Yes it does, and I swam the length. I got to swim in the deep end."

We went to Grandpa's house and changed into our dry clothes. I went outside to see if Jon or Rodney, who lived next door, were home. They had a big tricycle with a great big wheel in the front. It was much more fun than our little trikes.

A high hedge separated Jon and Rodney's house from Grandpa's house. Jon and Rodney's daddy worked for the electric company and drove a company truck. When Grandma was alive, she made sure there was an opening in the hedge so she could visit Jon and Rodney's mom.

I remembered going to Jon and Rodney's house one day. Grandma and Auntie Annette were sitting at the kitchen table. When Auntie Annette saw our muddy feet track across the kitchen floor, she said, "You outta be skinned alive!" She just meant we shouldn't walk into other people's houses with muddy feet, but Johnny wasn't sure.

That afternoon when we were home playing in "the hole," Johnny spotted Jon and Rodney's dad driving up our lane. He was driving slowly, doing a routine check on the electrical wires. Then he drove up to the house to check the electric meter, but Johnny was sure he was hunting for him. He ran to the house, and hid in the basement until Mr. Hagen drove away. Later we learned that threatening something like that wasn't to be taken literally. It was just words to let you know you really should wipe your feet before walking in the house.

Johnny and I finally found Jon and Rodney's tricycle. Just as we started riding it up the sidewalk the six o'clock fire siren wailed and Mom drove up. It was time to go to Uncle Bud and Auntie Annette's house for a cookout with Uncle Homer.

Auntie Annette was a good cook. She prepared vegetable salads, fruit salads, and meatless macaroni casseroles for Homer. She made a white cake with her famous thick fudge frosting.

Cousin Jeff and I helped each other get on the little bicycle. I learned to ride it last time we were there when Auntie Annette gave Mom a permanent in her hair. I used the porch step to help me climb on. I couldn't turn the bike, and I could only get off when I crashed. Jeff had learned to step on the peddle and swing his leg over. I watched.

Then he let me try. I practiced turning, but couldn't get the bicycle to turn all the way around without falling.

After supper Annette busied herself in the kitchen. She mixed vanilla ice cream and strawberry soda-pop in the mixing bowl. Her electric mixer whined as she created the tastiest shake I had ever had in my life. We sat on the steps and slowly ate the thick, pink dessert.

Uncle Homer left at the end of the week. I was sad. It would be a whole year before he came back to visit us.

Uncle Homer and Daddy

Chapter 13
The Slab

Daddy had spent the past several days in the field cutting the hay with the tractor-pulled farm mower. Now that the hay was sun dried, it was ready to be raked and loaded into the truck so it could be hauled back to the barn. Behind the barn Grandpa and Daddy would build huge haystacks with the loose hay, and the cows would be well fed throughout the winter months once again.

Farm hand in Hayfield

Daddy and David put tall wooden racks on the dump truck so they could carry as much hay as possible. The old hay rake with rounded tines had once been pulled by a team of work horses, but now Daddy hooked it to the old pickup truck. Paul drove the pickup slowly, staying in first gear. As he went around the field the rake clattered noisily behind, gathering the loose hay. Once the rake was full, he pulled the long hemp rope that reached from the rake to the cab of the pick-up truck. The tines lifted, depositing the hay it had gathered. The tines fell back down and raked the hay to collect another load.

Daddy drove the John Deere tractor. He had replaced the farmhand's metal scoop that he used to clean out the barn with the fork hay loader. The long wooden tines slid under the mounds of hay collected by the rake. The hydraulic lift raised the hay high above the racks on the dump truck, and, as the fork tilted, the hay slid into the truck box. David and Grandpa stood in the back of the truck with pitchforks, redistributing the hay into the corners of the box so more hay could be added. Once he filled the truck bed, David drove back to the barn and dumped the load close to the spot where they planned to build the haystacks.

Grandpa and Paul building a haystack

It was a hot day, and the kitchen was unbearably hot as Mom was canning chokecherry jelly and syrup. She squeezed the juice from the boiled, sour chokecherries, and then boiled the juice with sugar to make syrup for pancakes and waffles. She added pectin to some of the juice to make chokecherry jelly.

I hid from the heat in the cool basement, looking at comic books and snacking from a can full of freshly-picked garden peas that I had snuck from the pea patch. As I opened each pod and popped the sweet peas into my mouth, I paged through all the Richie Rich and Casper comic books.

The comic books didn't cost much, as the storekeeper tore the covers off of the unsold books and returned them to the suppliers. He let us have the coverless books for just a few pennies apiece. We bought them with our allowance money. Sometimes, when there were a lot of unsold comic books, the storekeeper would give Daddy a whole box of books for us to enjoy. We read and reread Archie, Wendy, Spooky, Casper, Red Hot, Superman, Richie Rich, and Dot and Lotta.

I went upstairs and asked Mom for a drink. She let me have a "Fizzie". A "Fizzie" looked like a colored Alka-Seltzer tablet, and came in a variety of flavors. As a tablet dissolved it turned the water in a glass into the color of the flavor we chose. Like pop, the drink popped and fizzed in our noses as we drank.

Grandpa drove up in the truck and David and Paul jumped out and ran inside.

"Let's go swimming," David suggested.

It was over 100 degrees outside so Dad said the boys could go home. He would load the truck himself, and Grandpa would drive the pickup with the rake.

"Come on, Mom! Let's go swimming!" we pleaded.

Mom finally agreed, and, as she finished pouring paraffin wax to seal the jelly and syrup jars, Carolyn helped us gather our swimming suits and towels. David found a couple good black inner-tubes to float on, and Paul filled a thermos jug with ice water. Johnny and I packed some homemade oatmeal-raisin cookies in waxed-paper sandwich bags for a snack.

On hot days like this, even Mom enjoyed cooling off in the water. She didn't like wearing a bathing suit in public, so preferred to swim in the river instead of the pool at the park. With the heat wave, the town pool would be too crowded, anyway.

We all climbed into the station wagon and headed for "the slab", one of our favorite swimming holes. The concrete slab was once part of the road that crossed the Poplar River near Scobey. It now served as a dam, backing up the river enough to form a quiet, not-too-deep pool. It used to be a popular swimming spot for the whole community, but now that the public pool in the Scobey Park was available, we rarely had to share the beach with anyone else.

Paul and David could do acrobatic stunts at the river, and it was shallow enough on the slab that Johnny and I could splash and have a great time.

Our station wagon lumbered slowly over the neglected road to the river. Mom drove around one pothole, just to be jostled by the next.

The river was low, as it normally is by late summer, but we didn't mind. We raced to the water, and David and Paul dove into the deeper pool as Johnny and I played in the shallow water on the cement slab.

Mom sat in the open car door, rubbing on tanning lotion in hopes of blocking some of the sun's rays from her fair skin. After she tucked the last red curl under her swimming cap, she waded in gingerly, getting used to the coolness of the water. Then she started swimming in circles on her back.

David and Paul did somersaults in the water and held contests to see who could stay underwater the longest. Carolyn stood on her hands and did acrobatics in the water.

"Let's see who can skip a rock the farthest," David challenged everyone.

Carolyn and Paul accepted the challenge and hunted for smooth, flat rocks. When they each had a nice pile of potentially winning rocks, they took turns. It seemed that no matter how far Paul and Carolyn could skip a rock, David's always went farther.

I felt bad that Daddy and Grandpa had to work, but Daddy didn't like swimming. He said he swam like a rock.

As I sat in the shallow-water I realized that, no matter how many skips David or Paul got out of a flat rock, the rock sank every time, just like Daddy.

After two fun-filled hours, Mom said it was time to go home. I didn't want to.

"What's that on your back?" Johnny squealed, pointing at me.

"O-ma-gosh!" David exclaimed. "It's a bloodsucker!"

I screamed and ran from the water to Mom. "Get it off! Get it off!"

Swimming at the Slab

Mom was just as squeamish as I was over such things, but she reached over to detach it from my back. David came to the rescue, and, as he pulled the slug-like bloodsucker, it stretched until it came loose. Then he said, "Oh, look! There's one between your toes, too."

I was so terrified that I could hardly breathe. Paul helped pull two more off me, and Johnny had three on his feet and legs. Now I was truly ready to go home. I didn't argue any more. It was time to go!

Chapter 14
Barbecue Grill and Storms

In spite of the blood suckers, we were refreshed from the swim in the river. The thermometer read 110 degrees. In the house it was even hotter because of Mom's canning project. Mom decided it was just too hot to cook. She told David to get the grill out of the coal shed and put it together. As he screwed the legs onto the grill pan, Johnny and Paul scraped a bucket of rocks off the driveway to use as the layer under the charcoal.

Carolyn and Mom mixed the onions and seasonings into the home-butchered hamburger meat, and formed thick patties to be grilled for supper. I opened a box of twin-bagged potato chips and Johnny helped me find a couple tubs of Mom's home-baked beans in the freezer in the basement.

Carolyn cut the left-over boiled potatoes in chunks as mom chopped onions and celery and mixed together mayonnaise, pickle juice and seasonings for potato salad.

"I'm going to get the cows," David said. He knew chores had to be done before we could eat supper. He took his .22 rifle with him in case he saw any gophers.

The ground squirrels, always referred to as gophers, were everywhere at this time of year, and some of the fields were badly damaged from these pests.

"I'll give you a big surprise if you get a gopher," I promised.

He disappeared over the hill in search of the cows. Fifteen minutes later he came back with the three milk cows and three dead gophers on a binder string.

"I got one more, but it fell down the gopher hole," he announced proudly. "What's my surprise, Kathy? I get one surprise for each gopher!"

"You gotta come here!"

He came to the barnyard gate and I grabbed his neck and kissed him quickly four times.

"No fair!" he yelled as he wiped my kisses off with his shoulder, his hands still full with his gun, and the string of gophers. "You gotta give me a real surprise!"

"Did you expect a kiss?" I asked.

"No!"

"Then it was a real surprise!"

I loved to trick David. He did not like anything "girly", so I often chased him with perfume, tried to kiss him, and tease him about girls in his class.

Teasing David with Girly Perfume

David and Paul went to the barn to milk the cows.
Sam, the border collie jumped in the cow's water tank.
"Poor dog is hot too!" David said.

Mom doused the charcoal with lighter fluid. The
coals flared up at first, and then just sat there. Finally, they
turned white and hot and were ready to be spread out to
cook the hamburgers. David and Paul finished the milking
chores, and Daddy and Grandpa cleaned up in the basin
as we set the food on the table. Once the hamburgers
were cooked Carolyn bellowed, "Come and get it before
we throw it to the cats!"

Daddy, Grandpa, and Mom sat in the kitchen with two
fans blowing straight at them, but the rest of us loaded our
plates and went outside to find places to sit on the porch
or on the hood of the car. The temperature was beginning

to cool slightly, and the scent of fresh hay and good food blended to make the smell of summer.

Mom brought out two bags of marshmallows. We impaled the marshmallows on long two-pronged utensils that Daddy had made for this purpose by twisting wires together, and held them over the red-hot coals, being careful not to start them on fire, and browning them just right.

The sun disappeared over the horizon, and we sat in the gloaming trying to guess what the weather would be like tomorrow.

David recited: "Red sky at night, sailor's delight. Red sky in the morning, sailor's take warning."

Tonight, the sky was orange and pink, with yellow and purple and rays of gold shining around the huge, puffy clouds. In the distance we could hear the rumbling of thunder. The colorful clouds formed a large mushroom at the top, and glowed as the lightning scrambled back and forth among the massive approaching thunder heads.

We had to extinguish the fire in the grill before we went inside, as a wind storm could blow sparks or hot coals into the dry grass and start a dangerous prairie fire. David filled an empty milk pail with water. The hot coals made a zinging sound like passing missiles as he dropped them into the cold water with the barbecue tongs. The sizzles sounded the end to a perfect day.

The storm that struck a short time later was violent, and a vicious wind rattled the windows as rain pounded on the roof. Dixie and her pup, Cookie, forced their way through the door and hid under the kitchen table. David ran inside after putting the grill away. Mom and Dad scrambled to put the cans and buckets stored in the corner of the boys' room under the leaks in the ceiling. The electric water-pump wouldn't run in the event of a power outage so Carolyn filled pitchers and jugs with water. David found the candles and oil lamps, and Paul and Johnny rounded up the flashlights.

When we had completed our tasks we gathered in the recently-added sun porch and watched the storm through the windows. Mom set up her new twin lens reflex camera to photograph the lightning as it danced on the horizon.

I was terrified of the loud crashes of thunder. Daddy had taught the older children about nature, with scientific explanations.

"Thunder is just the air slamming together after the super-hot lightning bolt cuts through the air. It's nothing to be afraid of," Paul explained.

"If you count after you see a flash of lightning you can tell how far away it is," David added. "If you can count to seven, it's a whole mile away."

At the next flash of lightning, we all counted. "One, two, three, four, five, six, seven, eight."... BOOM!

"See? It's over a mile away," Carolyn said as she hugged me tight.

"Lightning puts nitrogen back in the soil," Daddy lectured. "Without lightning, the quality of the wheat wouldn't be as high."

BOOM!

A sudden bolt of lightning lit up the sky, immediately followed by a loud crash of thunder, and the lights went out. We all screamed, even Carolyn and David. I cried and hid myself in Mom's dress.

"That one was right here!" David exclaimed.

Paul and Johnny turned on the flashlights, and Daddy got the matches to light the candles and kerosene lamps. The power outage would most likely last until sometime tomorrow, so Daddy said it was time to go to bed.

The rain came down with a steady beat, and the thunder rumbled in the distance as it led the storm away. We dressed in our pajamas by candlelight and gathered in the kitchen. Mom opened the entry and kitchen windows, and a cool breeze chased out the heat of the day.

The soft glow of the oil lamp flickered, and made our shadows dance on the wall. Daddy took one of the left-over marshmallows, and roasted it over the chimney of the oil lamp. It turned perfectly golden-brown. I felt sick from all the roasted marshmallows I had already eaten, so I didn't want any more.

The steady patter of rain continued, but the rumble from the thunder grew distant. Mom tucked me into my crib and kissed me good-night and we said our prayers.

I buried my face in my pink gingham doggie, and knew it would soon be morning. I wasn't scared anymore.

Daddy helped Mom unfolded the couch to prepare their bed, and Dad reminisced of his own childhood. He told Mom that his mother lit the polished oil lamp each evening and any work had to be done by its dim glow once the sun went down. They rarely stayed up late. Electricity changed their habits and the habits of our whole society. Electric lights made night time seem like day time.

I thought how long ago it was since Daddy was a little boy. And now I was his little girl, and he was the dad. As I closed my eyes and drifted off to sleep, I was glad I was the little girl, and I wouldn't be a grown-up for a long, long time.

Prairie